Reasons for Writing Poetry

EDUARDO CHIRINOS (Lima, Peru, 1960), an internationally
acclaimed voice in Latin American letters, is the author of sixteen
books of poetry as well as volumes of academic criticism, numerous
essays, translations, and children's books. His most recent
poetry title, *While the Wolf Is Around,* won the Generation of '27
International Poetry Prize, Spain, 2009. He is Professor of Spanish at
the University of Montana.

Reasons for Writing Poetry

EDUARDO CHIRINOS

Translated by

G. J. RACZ

S
SALT

LONDON

PUBLISHED BY SALT PUBLISHING
Dutch House, 307–308 High Holborn, London WC1V 7LL United Kingdom

Salt Publishing 2011

Printed and bound in the United States by Lightning Source Inc.

Typeset in Swift 9.5 / 13

ISBN 978 1 84471 521 3 paperback

1 3 5 7 9 8 6 4 2

for Jannine

Contents

Acknowledgements

Some of the translations in this volume have been published before, in slightly different form, in the following venues: *Another Chicago Magazine, Asheville Poetry Review, Beacons, The Carolina Quarterly, The Dirty Goat, Downtown Brooklyn, Hampden-Sydney Poetry Review, International Poetry Review, METAMORPHOSES, The Montana Association of Language Teachers Bulletin, Mr. Knife, Miss Fork, Nimrod, Northwest Review, Oval, Poet Lore, Review: Latin American Literature and Arts, Revista de poesía Prometeo, Seneca Review, Thorny Locust, Torre de papel, West View, Witness, Xavier Review* and *Zoland Poetry: An Annual of Poems, Translations & Interviews*.

In addition, the following translations (again, in slightly different form) were published in the chapbook *Crónicas de un ocioso/Chronicles of a Man of Leisure*, Carpeta de Poesía Luz Bilingüe N° 5, winner of Luz Bilingual Publishing, Inc.'s 1998 Poetry Translation Contest: "A Poem for Groucho, the One with the Moustache," "Twenty-five Years of Life for a Man," "Sea Stories," "Three Domestic Poems," "Christmas in Bavaria, 1986," "Dream of Sirens," "The Rain."

For further information on the references made in this collection, please see the *Notes* section, pp. 159–161.

"No, the Sphinx Doesn't Want an Answer": The Poetics of Eduardo Chirinos

"There is in Chirinos," Álvaro Salvador perceptively states on the front inside flap of the poet's *Abecedario del agua* (*The Water's ABC's*), "within all that seemingly grandiloquent staging, a humble and quite human lucidity characteristic of the Latin American tradition and, more concretely, of the Peruvian, a lucidity closer, in truth, to Vallejo or Quechuan poetry than to canonized European discourses. The transculturation of which Rama spoke is presented in these poems in a natural and admirable manner" (all translations from the Spanish are mine). Not surprisingly, given a body of work undertaken in earnest when the poet was only seventeen and which currently consists of no fewer than sixteen books, those remarking upon Chirinos's three decades of literary output can now even speak of stages in his oeuvre and of an inevitable evolution in his poetics. Born in Lima in 1960, Chirinos is widely considered one of the most important members of Peru's 80's Generation, a group that came of age after a decade of military governments in a socio-political climate seeking a return to normalcy amid the emergence of terrorist violence by the Communist insurgent *Sendero Luminoso* (Shining Path). His singular voice and vision have, by almost all accounts, outlasted the more local concerns of a poetic movement characterized by a focus on language, however debased its ability to correlate to the realities of Peruvian politics and life. As Ramón Cote notes on that same inside flap, "Without being grandiloquent or abusing Culture with a capital C, Chirinos has managed to incorporate the great themes of literature into his poetry—life, death, and love—and to call them by their own names."

No matter what his subject or theme, and though varied they are signature—the return to childhood, the vagaries of memory, the alternative reality of dream, a fascination with animals, the utility of seeing and hearing, water as vital force, the poetic tradition, the writer's place in aesthetic history, the creative act itself, and the never-ending search for originality through innovative expression — Chirinos configures works in which, as José Antonio Mazzotti, another member of the 80's Generation, adeptly points out in reference to *Archivo de huellas digitales* (*Fingerprint File*): "It is suggested that modernity carries its own destruction within itself and that modern eloquence thus loses force before a social reality where there no longer appears to be any way out and failure seems the only constant" (in Vich). Writing broadly of the aesthetics of Chirinos's first phase — which encompasses the seven poetic volumes *Cuadernos de Horacio Morell* (*The Notebooks of Horacio Morell*, 1981, reissued 2006), *Crónicas de un ocioso* (*Chronicles of a Man of Leisure*, 1983), *Archivo de huellas digitales* (*Fingerprint File*, 1985), *Rituales del conocimiento y del sueño* (*Rituals of Knowledge and Dream*, 1987), *El libro de los encuentros* (*The Book of Encounters*, 1988), *Canciones del herrero del arca* (*Songs of the Ark's Blacksmith*, 1989), and *Recuerda, cuerpo...* (*Remember, Body...*, 1991) — Diego Otero asserts: "Eduardo Chirinos's creative development...is, paradoxically, an example of insularity as well as a lesson in permanence, ideological tendency, and rigor. Taken together, the first half of his work stands in surprising contrast to that of the rest of his generation (which took street language to an extreme and spoke loudly and outrageously of marginality). Chirinos's poetry is meticulous, tinged with nuances from and nods toward the classics. In its finest moments, his work appears to be a sort of tranquil and melancholy epic of everyday existence" (9).

José Miguel Oviedo, one of the most astute commentators on Chirinos's work to date, rightly views this poet's "most mature production coinciding roughly with his exile in the United States" (*La poesía*, 652). Referring to the volumes of poetry beginning with *El equilibrista de Bayard Street* (*The Bayard Street Tightrope Walker*, 1998) and proceeding through *Abecedario del agua* (2000), *Breve historia de la música* (*A Brief History of Music*, 2001), *Escrito en Missoula* (*Written in Missoula*, 2003), *El Fingidor* (*The Faker*, 2003), *No tengo ruiseñores en el dedo* (*No Nightingales on My Finger*, 2006), *Humo de incendios lejanos* (*The Smoke of Distant Fires*, 2009), *Catorce formas de melancolía* (*Fourteen Types of Melancholy*, 2009) and *Mientras el lobo está* (*While the Wolf Is Around*, 2010), Oviedo observes of this (for the moment) second stage of poetic output: "This phase...would be enough for Chirinos to be considered one of the outstanding [Peruvian] poets to have come along in the last thirty years... His vision unfailingly contains the emotional immediacy of the expressed in complete harmony with the perceived. There is a music to his verse, a precise timbre that vibrates with a captivating resonance; this music is not mere adornment tacked onto what he is saying, but a substantive part of his poetry and the primary reason for its aesthetic value" (*La poesía*, 653). Víctor Vich's cogent remarks on Chirinos's use of language merit an ever lengthier citation here. In the poetry of Eduardo Chirinos, Vich asserts,

> there is a very clear awareness that language has been socially exhausted and that this running to waste constitutes — in addition to a certain societal uselessness — the most conscious literary dissatisfaction in his writing. This poetry no longer conceives of language as "pure" and "isolated," as something violence and absurdity have left unscathed. We don't find in its images any urge to represent reality without an awareness of the mediation language itself presupposes. Therefore, the division that pits language against the world, idealizing the former to the detriment of the latter, never occurs. On the contrary, the two generate a total co-identification in which the failure of (either) one leads to the uselessness of the other. In this sense, it is important to begin by saying that, in Eduardo Chirinos's poetry, beauty no longer appears as a value loaded with transcendental and idealistic signifieds but as an incomprehensible sign that begins to have very little to say.

Thankfully for both scholars and lovers of Latin American poetry, discerning critics such as those cited above have been less hesitant to categorize and extol Chirinos's significant poetic achievement than the author himself has. Chirinos routinely declines to codify his vast output with facile self-categorization. In the Introduction to his unpublished *Cuaderno Rojo* [*Red Notebook*], for example, a collection of the first half of his complete poetical works, Chirinos demurs as follows: "Now that I am writing these lines, I realize how difficult it is to present poetry without giving in to the temptation of propounding a poetics. I prefer to let the poems construct their own, even at the risk of their going adrift and capsizing in the attempt." Evoking the fatalistic quality that writing poetry has for him, Chirinos confesses in the Introduction to *The Water's ABC's*: "It just happens that, after all these years, I still don't feel like I know what I am 'trying to express' in my poems. They are smarter than I, and end up expressing me, while I allow myself to be expressed with alarming passivity" (7). This reverse phenomenon is no doubt what Vich has in mind when he writes that, for Chirinos, "poetic composition becomes ritualized in a kind of rite of initiation through which the poet is held spellbound before a superior force that, both within and outside of his being, attracts and calls him. Poetry as an indecipherable entity emerges from the individual subject who then becomes the one who endeavors to approach it." This insight may help the reader empathize with the speaker of Chirinos's "Christmas in Bavaria, 1986," who, after contrasting a holiday spent in Germany with another in Peru, ends by declaring: "I never liked Christmas, I must confess./ I don't know why I am writing this poem."

Chirinos's preoccupation with linguistic efficacy manifests itself most consistently through the fear of poetic cliché present throughout his oeuvre. Esperanza López Parada, for one, points out how "[s]uddenly, the abhorrent likelihood that something has already been said and the discomforting feeling that nothing new can be said jump into the tranquil lake of his poetic diction" (11). As the speaker of "You've Knelt Naked on the Flagstones" laments, "You've plagiarized a line, Edward, Edward." For a writer whose own experiences are so deeply entrenched in the world's poetic tradition,

Chirinos, Vich affirms, seeks to "find images from his personal past, the literary canon or what I have defined as an 'intertextual I' with the purpose of ritualizing the most traditional knowledge on the basis of inherited images." Indeed, intertextual references in the form of direct citations, subtle line variations or epigraphs may be found of the following poets (and, no doubt others) in the present volume alone: Horace, Robert Duncan, Lautréamont, Dylan Thomas, Homer, Ennius, William Blake, Cesare Pavese, César Vallejo, Peter Huchel, José Emilio Pacheco, Constantine Cavafy, Martín Adán, Vicente Aleixandre, William Shakespeare, Pedro Calderón de la Barca, René Char, William Carlos Williams, Robert Lowell, José Asunción Silva, Rubén Darío, Zhang Kejiu, Edgar Allen Poe, W. B. Yeats, Pablo Neruda, Dante, Ernesto Cardenal, Ezra Pound, Virgil, Robert Bly, Juan Gelman, Umberto Saba, Vicente Huidobro, George Seferis, Lucian Blaga, Osip Mandelstam, Juan Larrea, and Lucretius. In light of this daunting weight of aesthetic influence, which the poet prefers to dub "affinities" (Guerrero), Chirinos's speakers are understandably wary of falling back on trite symbols and utterances. The speaker of "Raritan Blues," for example, ends the poem on this note: "They say the river is life and the sea death./ Here is my elegy:/ a river is a river/ and death an affair that shouldn't concern us." In "Daughters of the Lonesome Isle," one reads à la Gertrude Stein that "a lake/ is a lake/ is a lake." On the topic of roses, the speaker of "The Conch and the Rose" states that "you cannot stop looking at the Rose" (written here with the appropriate capital letter) because "[i]ts discreet stench moves you." "Letters that Arrive without Fanfare" makes a similarly withering mention of "so many roses wheedled by time." After a self-consciously "standard" set-up in the unpoetically titled prose piece "Just an Average Dog," the speaker of this poem states in an attempt to recuperate his own language's referential potential, "The sky was clear (that's a lie)...." In "Love and the Sea," after noting "a nubile body on the red carpet," the speaker asks between parentheses: "What is a nubile body doing on the red carpet?" Examples abound. The speaker of "La Solitudine," after indulging in the particularly ethereal phrasing "in my heart there is only rain," brings himself back down to earth by asking: "Why/ am I writing the word *heart*? I've never/ written the word *heart* before." One of the two voices in "The Book of My Life or My Conversations with Saint Teresa of Ávila," having heard the other recount a battle between demons and angels, inquires: "why are you talking about angels? i've never seen one ever." On the opposite side of the same coin, Chirinos's speakers can also demonstrate a metalingual affinity for the well-turned phrase. The speaker of "Mortally Wounded Okapi," for instance, opens this poem by confessing: "For years now, I have been hounded by the title/ 'Mortally Wounded Okapi'." Exhibiting a similar tendency, the speaker of "The Color of Nightfall" closes this piece by observing: "It has taken centuries to say 'orange nightfall'."

As a counterbalance, then, to language's diminished status as referential system, many of Chirinos's poems employ repetition as a kind of *pseudo* refrain. A phrase or line repeated (sometimes more than once) within a Chirinos work typically provides an internal structure that reinforces the (deflated) linguistic constitution of the aesthetic object while bracing the reader for a conclusion that does not always ring sweepingly poetic. This strategy can range from the simple redundancy of "Edward, Edward" in "You've Knelt Naked on the Flagstones" (inspired by a traditional Scottish ballad) to the more imbricated patterns of "Twenty-five Years of Life for a Man," in which what the child does "[i]n his solitude" and which concepts "go together and are inseparable" make the reader constantly reassess the work's poetic significance. If the ominous verse "[H]ow many things lie in wait for us when death is on the prowl" resonantly punctuates the first five stanzas of "Sermon on Death," and the last line of "A Theory of Sight After a Poem by Seferis" brings the reader back to the first with a splendid commentary on the act of poetic creation, the line "[R]eturning is always a little sad" in "The Raccoons in Johnson Park" leads to this less than illuminating coda about these little animals with their "cartoon-thief masks": "I'll see them again soon at the zoo,/ rummaging for food in the garbage/ or splattered by cars on the road." Oviedo expounds on this elemental feature of Chirinos's oeuvre most accurately when he states:

> Chirinos opens his inner world to us by using a repertoire of
> recurrent symbols and elements: glances, words, silences, light,
> the sea, dreams. He handles them by relying on a system of
> reiterations and variants, of anaphoric formulas and *ritornellos*,
> of echoes and doublings of the poetic phrase within a line or
> through enjambment, which create a sense of expectation and
> rhythmic familiarity. Frequently, the poem is a subtle game that
> begins with only a few of these elements, continues with an
> unfolding in which they combine with others, and finally folds
> in upon itself by returning to the beginning. The result is a
> circularity analogous to the way in which a musical composi-
> tion presents its motifs and then goes about incorporating new
> chords and tonalities into its central theme. (Música, 18)

What remains quite remarkable, then, given this suspicion of
language's power to convey unambiguous meaning, is the near
critical consensus regarding the pleasing lyricism of the whole
of Chirinos's work, a quality notable even in translation. "His
voice is melodious, deliberate, cadenced, serene, and reflexive,
which sets him apart from the poets of his generation for whom
it was common to seek out dissonance and colloquialism (which
is perfectly legitimate)," Oviedo opines (Música, 18). Referring to
Chirinos's "Brandenburgische Konzert N° 2," although he might
well have been speaking of the poet's collective oeuvre, Vich states:
"Chirinos is lyric but nonetheless narrational, mythic but nonethe-
less historical." When López Parada notes that "Chirinos's poetic
output contains a high percentage of indescipherable or reticent
writing...[such that] the poetic act is transformed into the art of
insinuation or imprecise content, the exquisite art of only naming
things in part but with an elegant reserve" (11), she touches upon
the poet's own belief that the silences in his work might well be
considered a better reflection of the turmoil of his times than the
more overtly politicized poetry of his contemporaries. Others,

such as Gustavo Buntinx, describe Chirinos's voice as "mythic, oracular, prophetic...emerging from the other side of clairvoyance, almost from disenchantment." It is no wonder, since so many of Chirinos's poems feature oracles, prophets, or figures simply speculating about the future, among them the conquistadors in "A Hot Wind Blows Over Desert Dunes," Daniel in "Like the Ice of a Dark Passion (Nebuchadnezzar's Dream)," and the title personae in "Cassandra's Monologue" and "Tiresias Speaks." All of which brings this Introduction to a conclusion with a discussion of the mask.

"Where there is discourse, there are masks," Chirinos cagily affirms in his interview with Buntinx, "It's just that masking in poetry takes on greater force." Over his thirty-year career, Chirinos has largely shed the device of speaking through a fictive persona that he initiated with his first book of poetry, *Cuadernos de Horacio Morell*, which purported to be the writings of this invented writer discovered after his suicide. Too transparent to be a heteronym in the manner of Fernando Pessoa's counterparts and near alter egos Alberto Caeiro, Ricardo Reis or Álvaro de Campos, Horacio Morell subsequently yielded to other historical, mythical, and literary figures to whom Chirinos has, over the years, lent his voice. These include, of course, not only his forays into the imaginary cognitive worlds of Maecenas's cook ("The Best of the Poets of Rome"), Leon Trotsky ("Russian Legends"), Ophelia ("The Fable of Ophelia and Segismund"), and others, but of the wholesale inhabiting of such figures as the ark's blacksmith and the Bayard Street tightrope walker. If Horacio Morell was, as Chirinos explains, "[a] fiction of my own fears, the secret of my own failures" (Hermoza M., 52), invented because the adolescent poet "naively believed that those poems were going to reveal [him] naked before the world" (Ildefonso), these comments characteristically do not go far enough to illuminate Chirinos's ultimate transformation of the device from fictitious mouthpiece to psycholinguistic point of view to dialogic mechanism. Casting a backward glance upon his singular poetic output in the final section of *No tengo ruiseñores en el dedo* (see, for example, both "Horacio Morell" and "No Nightingales on My Finger"),

Chirinos, as evident, too, in the last four poems of this volume from *Humo de incendios lejanos*, has most recently introduced second and third voices in fashioning a complex polyphony of competing world views. As the reader progresses through this first English-language selection of Chirinos's work, s/he would do well to ask the questions that continue to haunt Vich, namely: "Who is speaking in this poetry?" and "From where are the voices that we hear coming?"

GREGARY J. RACZ
Brooklyn, NY, August 1, 2010

Works Cited

Chirinos, Eduardo. *Abecedario del agua.* Valencia: Pre-Textos, 2000.

———. Interview with Gustavo Buntinx. Unpublished.

———. Interview with Omar Guerrero. *Revista El hablador* n° 6. Dec. 2004. http://www.elhablador.com/chirinos.htm.

———. Interview with Luis Miguel Hermoza M. *Revista Paralelo Sur.* Dec. 2006. 52-53.

———. Interview with Miguel Ildefonso. "El regreso de Horacio Morell." *Revista Letras S5.com.* http://www.letras.s5.com/archivoildefonso.htm.

———. "Sobre el *Cuaderno Rojo* y el *Cuaderno Azul.*" Introduction. *Cuaderno Rojo (Poemas, 1978-1991).* By Eduardo Chirinos. Unpublished book.

López Parada, Esperanza. "Decir como si fuera por primera vez." *ABC Cultural.* 27 Jan. 2001. 11.

Otero, Diego. "El miedo y la belleza." *Dominical de El Comercio.* 8 Jul. 2001. 9.

Oviedo, José Miguel, ed. *La poesía del siglo XX en Perú.* Madrid: Editorial Visor—Casa de América, 2008. 651-78.

———. "Música verbal." *ABC de las Artes y las Letras.* 5 Aug. 2006. 18-19.

Vich, Víctor. "Asalto al canon: Sobre la poética de Eduardo Chirinos." Unpublished essay.

from *The Notebooks of Horacio Morell*

Beatus Ille (Natural History)

The calf mooing and chewing her cud in the Rímac River valley
knows nothing of the teat cups they'll hang on her udder
if she disturbs the normal ruminant imbalance
between the dairy cows and funny little calves of the Rímac River
    valley.
This we know and, truth to tell, it doesn't pain us
as we are cheered to hear of the calf's promotion to the stables
and even applaud the injustice committed
when she is forced to squirt her milk into bottles
fresh for our consumption
with its distinctly rugged cowboy taste,
a few days' growth of beard and all that.
But this is not at all important here
since we aren't interested in these cows
but (as we have said) in the ones mooing and chewing their cud
    in the Rímac River valley,
those whose spots may reveal the presence of ticks or lash marks,
aspiring neither to be fattened up nor privately owned.
Still one fine day you'll see
the cowherds brushing (or bathing) the calf to sell at a good price
with the aim of moving just that much closer to Lima.
The poor thing won't know her udder is no longer hers,
won't know about the stable or the expert hands of some white-
    smocked boy.
She will only moo and continue chewing her cud,
using her tail to brush away the flies from the wide-eyed children.

A Poem for Groucho, the One with the Moustache

Comrade Groucho:

You're no card-carrying party member
and, frankly, I doubt that you're militant
but my sister (the oldest one)
never watched any of your movies
because she thought they were about socialism
and she doesn't care for socialism
(or anything else bearing your horrible cousin's name).
I, though, loyal to the man,
made theatre forays for days and days (all useless surveys) but I've
    been thinking:
maybe if he weren't so horrible
he wouldn't scare so many of the bourgeoisie.
So I gave myself over to laughter
and to collecting stubs from the Opera
                    the Circus
                    the Races,

thinking I might find
the key to power.

The Giraffe and Bus Derby

So we spend all our time circling a shoe-print,
galloping along on a giraffe's back,
crashing into our own circumstances
and brandishing swords that might be radio antennae
or second-hand golf clubs.
Sometimes we sleep long owl nights
atop rocks that butt into the game,
opening the doors of our Swiss chalet to piss in the lake
and feed the giraffe as a reward for its benevolence.
Other times we prefer to retire without sleeping
and peruse some atlas, animal volume or book of poems,
looking a great deal like the clown in the Easter parade.
To break from routine you stand on your head
and look up the hardest word in the dictionary,
sticking your legs out the tallest building's top-floor window
and shouting it out
(all the while securing the saddle on your giraffe
in case people finally understand you
and you have to fly off to strange lands where you're not known).
If you are prevented from doing this,
you simply draw your face in the middle of the road
and make the cars swerve by brandishing a toy pistol.
But
should you emerge victorious this way
you will continue circling the shoe-print
or will have to set off on a trip.

So it is that the saddest thing in the world is having no name
to scribble on the back seat of the bus you're traveling on.

from *Chronicles of a Man of Leisure*

You aren't ashamed to be like the rest,
living in perpetual shadow,
caressing the rocks, yearning to be like them some day.
You're like a hollowed-out telephone full of inaudible words,
a placid stream where flocks of proud rats drink,
a dull knife chopping pointlessly at a block of wood.
A lazy wind carries off your flowers
as you try to flee the seeming confinement of your cell,
beautiful and spacious as the seven continents.
You've joined your neighbors in wild abandon,
a woman dripping down between your eyes
like the honey that sweetens and destroys us,
loving us unwittingly.
The rats will die in the end because they can't figure out the purpose
    of their species
and are happy to play in the garbage like all creatures great and
    what have you.
This is what allows them to be born, die and be born again
while you, a hollowed-out telephone in the wilderness,
inflict harm on the place and are a real pain,
a dull knife indifferent to words,
an ignorant man imprisoned in a country similarly imprisoned
where everything is entirely yours
as long as you don't come face to face with your eyes
and understand that it's too late now to give your sentence meaning.

The Dead Rocks

To ascertain whether a rock is really dead
you have only to observe it carefully.
This is hardly a difficult venture—
even a child can usually tell a dead rock from the others,
especially if the grass it's crushing turns yellow like the sun
and the clouds in the sky continue to lengthen
its shadow.

I've never had any respect for dead rocks.
What's more, I could never tell them from the live ones
though, whenever
I'd wander through the gorges,
I'd take along a backpack full of stones
so I could feed them
like a person tossing corn to church pigeons.

I was popular with the rocks.
When I conversed with them they'd look at me pensively,
never asking a single question,
just smiling shyly when I recited poems.
Sometimes I'd sit down on one
and lavish it with great affection
until I made it die a slow death.

Sometimes I'd throw the stones into the river
and they wouldn't even protest,
just stare at me and turn dark
until they disappeared forever.

I'd feel sad when this occurred
because it signaled the time for me to leave the dead rocks
until the next day. Or never.

Free Version of the Stanzas the Young Ali-Nur Recited Before Kutait the Gaoler on One of the Nights King Shahryar Listened Attentively to the Story of Sweet-Friend

Provinces in the South, provinces in the East, provinces in the West.
What lies ahead for me as I hide in these lands?
How often have I seen myself resting with a dead man's calm,
a torch's fake grandeur lighting the walls of a stone palace! How often
    have
sour wine and the pieces on a dark chessboard pounded in my head
like the vague memory of a solitary young woman strumming her lute!
I have observed at length the moon's distant movement
and know that man's designs are preordained.
Deliver me, Allah, from the wrath of my enemies.

I have dragged my body through the vastest expanses of solitude,
buried my head in my wife's breasts and cried at length,
freed birds from their bronze cages hanging on high
and fled the fury of merchants amid showerings of manure.
I have shaven off my beard so that I would not be recognized,
abandoned father, wife and children,
yoked oxen in the lowliest orchards of Damascus,
fled the uproar of the Moors with a daughter of their blood
and conspired against the Captain Major of the realm.

I know that man's designs are preordained.

Deliver me, Allah, from the wrath of my enemies, though the heat
    scorch
and condemn me to the infertility of the waters.
Deliver me, Allah, from the wrath of my enemies,
though I die like a blade of grass beneath the hooves of horses.

from *Fingerprint File*

Food for Fire
For Alberto Hernández

If you look you will see the salamander
— ROBERT DUNCAN

"If you look you will see the salamander."
It's true.
Leonardo saw figures that were stains upon a wall
and, piecing together the details one by one, dispelled doubt
until doubt took on form and form
the contours of a figure natural or strange.

Pisa, 1476.
Mist floats over the hills of Albani.
The scene is of a sheepfold and takes us back to our supreme
    ignorance,
the pillar of sand beside the sea.
Foam clings to the shore and is blown away by the wind.
Now you see the beach, the cool, salt beach strewn with crab shells —
if you look you will see the salamander —
the lighted residence at 15 rue Vivienne.

Paris, 1870.
Someone is writing with the confidence of a person who knows
    something.

"Hatred is stranger than you think,"
Lautréamont used to say. "It can't be explained,
like why a stick looks broken in the water."

It's true.
Lautréamont saw a metaphor for hatred
where others only see a stick in the water.

A Hot Wind Blows Over Desert Dunes

An homage to José María Arguedas and Pedro Cieza de León

"Don't think it's all sand and shingle here.
Toward the east where the Gran Cordillera rises, a wind blows so
    cold
it splits the lips and numbs the bones.
And don't let asthma or the humidity lower your spirits, either—
on the other side of the sandbank you'll see parched hills and
    narrow rivers
where no plant life grows and natural beauty is scant.
You may begin to lose heart, but will have to pull yourself
    together:
what did you leave behind in Spain that's worth the worry?
What's separation compared to the happiness you'll come by in
    this realm?
Be patient, bless the moment they said, 'It's a boy,'
for neither the iciest cold nor the most stifling heat will make
    you turn back.
Not even the hot wind that stirs and pounds the dunes will chase
    us from this land,
which will be ours some day."

(The Coast of Tumbez forwards has no Mountains,
and if there be any Ridges they are Naked, and all Rocky;
but the greatest Part is Sandy, and few Rivers fall into the Sea).

My heart beat weakly beneath the weight of a question: will my
    children and my children's children
ever live on this soil?
I spurred on my nag, holding tightly to its neck.
The weather was warm
and sweat dampened its hooves as they wended their skillful way
    over rocky ground,
trotting surefootedly in the dust.
My companion whistled an Andalusian tune and I thought of
    Jathib,
the old Moor who amused us with legends and card tricks.

"Ah!," he said, "the sun is burning brighter and we should rest,"
so we covered ourselves with blankets and slept a while.
When we awoke, a string of gulls flew over our heads.
"They could well be fish," I said.
Here the sea is the same color as the sky and I lost my bearings.
"I don't know where I am;
maybe we've made a big circle and aren't very far from where we
    set out."
"They're birds, and we're a hundred leagues south of Gorgona.
What are you afraid of?
This is not the first time I've passed through these parts and
    I can assure you we are no more than three days from our
    destination."

(The Coast, as I said before, is all free from Mountains,
being nothing but Sands and bare Rocky Crags.)

The next morning, we took a short detour to admire this ocean's
    waters once again.
The foam came up to our knees and thousands of tiny fish
    surrounded us,
skittish little fish that shone like colorful needles from their
    contact with the light.
"It's not the Mediterranean, but it will do for a swim," he said,
plunging his body into that frigid sea.
Then he walked toward me, holding out his hands, and said,
    "Look,
these are called *muymuys*."
Right then I understood why this sand is so coarse and unlike all
    others.

(The Water rises and falls here so much, that upon the Ebb,
the Coast is dry for above half a League,
and fills up again with the Flood.)

The sandy ground, all trampled as if by pigeon feet, was smoothed over by the wind.

My companion pointed to the Gran Cordillera and looked at me
    inquiringly.
With the conviction weariness confers, I said to him:
"I'm staying. This will be my land.
I'll choose my woman from among the warm flesh here and
    father my children upon her.
In the end they'll forget me because I mean so little.
Perhaps some day they'll return home from these heights as I
    have traveled from across the sea
and, before they make up their minds to inhabit these lands, will
    sit as I do
now: pale and embittered
like an animal from the frigid flatlands brought to the shore
over sands strange and burning hot."

Like the Ice of a Dark Passion
(Nebuchadnezzar's Dream)

In the fifth year of his reign, Nebuchadnezzar had a dream; and his spirit was troubled, and sleep left him. He ordered his magicians, enchanters, and astrologers summoned to explain this dream to him, yet none could interpret it. Only Daniel, who possessed learning and understanding in all arts and sciences, saw fit to let him speak, thereby uncovering the mystery in his words and remaining at the court of the king.

...the hot air frightened me,
air swaying like a bronze clapper, battering my body.
The pastures were covered with water and the seas surged.
I gazed upon the Chaldean ships about to be destroyed,
considering the sea monsters that perturbed geographers' minds
and the glory of my dead ancestors.

Then, the earth trembled with such fury the walls shook and
    tongues of fire fell upon my misfortuned head.

Fear is instinctive, I thought; there must be some animal in me.
Am I to live among the beasts and let my skin be damp with dew?
Am I to run on all fours and feed upon the grasses of the hills?
No refuge is possible
since everything impels me to consummate my own destruction
and gaze out upon the five thousand islands lying strewn like the
    remains of jellyfish.

That's when I saw my parents. I can remember it as clear as day:
she with her silver diadem and braid down her back,
he with his burnished face and curly beard.
The two floated by in absolute calm and seemed not to know
    each other.
They were dead.

She had long, slender legs. A downy bush appeared to join them below her womb while her breasts were round and ample. The air was hot. Fear tied my stomach in knots and kept me glued to the keyhole. There I discovered that I would love her forever, that I desired her with all my being and that the world might come to a halt if she stroked my hair until I succumbed to sleep.

The palace began to burn.
The curtains looked like torches from a hell that must have been
    very cold, like skin,
like the ice of a dark passion, like the fever devouring and
    consuming my body...

Visions like these are not common.
Good Arioch tells me you despise my food and scorn the favor of
    our gods. He tells me, too,
that vegetables are your fare and water your drink,
that you are noble and know the meaning of dreams.
Might you perchance reveal the mystery that torments my soul
    and troubles my senses?

This world is half the devil's and my own
— DYLAN THOMAS

And what will ye do wi' your tow'rs and your ha',
Edward, Edward?
— TRADITIONAL SCOTTISH BALLAD

You've knelt naked on the flagstones
and looked long at your shit, Edward, Edward.
Three days without food and you've emptied your body,
the waste resembling a docile animal at rest by the side of the road.
You are naked, Edward, Edward. You've awkwardly rubbed your
    crystal ball and seen nothing,
barely a rush of horses roaring down the trail,
barely your rotted bones floating in the sea.
You are alone, Edward, Edward.
Now is the time to close your eyes and scratch your nails on the
    mirror's hazy surface, time
to smash medallions and spit on portraits of B. de Portinari.

Your genitals are pointing south, Edward, Edward.
The impostor arrow scatters flocks of birds flying in the wrong
    direction
and you bring your palms together to kindle the fire.
That's the way the world is, Edward, Edward,
the world that makes of love an ear-splitting scream,
that makes of love a broken windowpane.

Half the world is yours and the other half the devil's, Edward,
    Edward,
but that half is a mesh of copper mail where empty
words hang like cardboard boxes waiting to be used.
You've plagiarized a line, Edward, Edward,
bent over your shit to pull up stakes and drive them in again,
looking at yourself pointlessly in the mirror

until you realized that now is the time to say a few words
in case the docile animal at rest by the side of the road should awaken
and be trampled.

from *The Book of Encounters*

"Twenty-five years of life for a man
make two lives for one who is fifty," my father used to say.
I remember it still.
I must have been nine or ten, an age when hours
transpire in a slow haze and every night
is a fleeting fade-to-black where dreams dwell.
(Sometimes memory preserves old dreams
that burn like torches offering light
while other times it calls for our hands,
looking to dunk them in ponds to search for prints.)

I found only the word — all else was denied me.
Dimwitted, I took a long while to understand that heavenuponearth
    is better than utopia, that heartfelt love is never impossible, that
    childhood bundles us off proudly then grabs hold.
What fate does the word have in store for those who are its chosen?
That's hard to say.
In his solitude the child masturbates and feels fear,
understanding that fear and pleasure go together and are inseparable.
In his solitude he discovers beauty and feels fear,
understanding that fear and beauty go together and are inseparable.
Then only the word remains,
a deep hole where smoke betrays its presence, its high flame
    touching us without burning.
Smoke is the sign preceding encounters, the errant ash whose fruit is
    the poem
because dream and poem always travel together
and are inseparable.

Childhood Revisited
(Corrales, Tumbes 1965)
For my brother Carlos

Dust and rocks on a dull brown landscape, smooth-coated donkeys
    and herons flying over the yellow grass.
Remember:
mist circling the walls of a medieval castle
and howling wolves at the foot of the hills.
The hero clutches his lance to jab at the poisonous fury of a dragon
whose small head peering out from behind a stone

                                        takes cover again,

deftly dodging the projectiles seeking to destroy it.
War cries, torn pants, grimy stains, Siegfried
with trimmed fingernails and dirty ears, Siegfried
between a six-o'clock snack and his lizard's tail.
"Don't worry, it'll grow back, like when you have your hair cut."

The sun parches the cows' dark tongues while toad
cadavers lie splattered along the trail.
(Ramírez would walk us home from school and charge at them.
"They have to die: they eat our fruit all day
then turn into cockroaches and bats at night.")

The sun rests on the curved surface of a gasoline truck.
Remember:
dust and rocks on a dull brown landscape, the white guts of pacas
    and the smell of tobacco drying.
Vacations were the far-off rumble of a jeep with toy soldiers and an
    old cemetery where we used to play amid death announcements
    and lime-coated niches,
the river we never crossed for fear of the iguanas and Siegfried's
    towel waving on the tip of a towering bamboo stalk.

They were vast beaches where the sand is tepid and white like a
    grandmother's thighs,
like the pale, bitter milk in which flies breathe their last.

The Best of the Poets of Rome

...but off you ran, indifferent, to the fields,
happy to eat on the coin of Maecenas
— HORACIO MORELL

An old cat yawns beneath the window and not a single cloud
    mars the pulchritude of the sky,
clean and expansive like an unfolded sheet.
It's hot outside
so the servants wave ostrich feathers to cool the chamber
of marble columns against which the youngest present recline.
There is Lycinius, thin and bent, biting his fingernails,
and Favonius, the author of obscure epigrams no one has read.
The lovely Marcia, too. She is not alone —
Vitelius, imperial leader of the Danubian legions, escorts her.
There are the old women, white-haired and wrinkled,
and the rosy-cheeked maidens with golden braids.
Diffugere nives, redeunt iam gramina campis...

In the kitchen the slaves are at work.
Maecenas serves up dishes of chicken with almonds,
fruits from the Orient and sweet wine from Campania.
"This smells like shit," the cook says.
Then a grave, melodious voice rises above the smoke.
A few timidly approach the room while others
take their chances behind the columns.
Who could resist such a noble cadence?
Sweet Phyllis leaves her chores to listen to so wondrous a voice.
Ne sit ancillae tibi amor pudori...

"Don't be so shocked, sweet Phyllis," the cook says.
"That man is from Venosa. I know him.
We played as boys in the town squares and gardens, hiked along
    streams and over mountains and walked to school together.
He was very shy and thin, then,
poor at reckoning sums but deft

at composing verses, which he relished showing his friends.
He never really had any, though.
He was always alone, dreaming of the women poets sang about,
bad at gymnastics and scornful of all games and sport.
In this he took after his father, a tax collector and fishmonger in
the plazas of Venosa.
I haven't seen him since then.
They say he served in Brutus's army and, after
the disaster, journeyed to Rome reduced to a beggar.
Ah, my old friend, what good did your poems do you
if now you beg alone in the streets?
Still, Jove lavished genius and stature upon him. His verses
delighted Virgil and he won Varro's friendship.
That's how he came to meet Maecenas.
He suddenly had at his disposal piles of money and an estate
where he would shut himself in to work. The shy young man
touched the comely Livia's breasts and became inflamed with love
for the divine Chloë
but sang the feats of Augustus like no other,
immortalizing so the memory of Maecenas.

Don't you forget it,
that short, fat man everyone looks upon with reverence and
respect, that man
whose mouth waters to taste our fine fare
is Horace, sweet Phyllis, the best of the poets of Rome."

from *Rituals of Knowledge and Dream*

Cassandra's Monologue

For Susana de Vivanco

I was very young when I rejected the god who offered me his body.
I spat angrily upon his sacred tongue,
insulting him as if he were the basest of mortals.
That is why I, who would relive my past in dreams,
now dream the terrible future of man.
No one believes me, it's true.
No magnificent sanctuaries honor me and no splendid statues of
    me are raised,
but some do listen in fear to my prophecies,
piously awaiting the high flame of my fate.
I know they scorn me, calling me the "Beguiler of Men,"
but what are men, anyhow?
Mere puppets in a story no one controls,
paltry arrows unaware of the tension in the bow.
I remember when I was a girl my parents left me behind in the
    temple
where sacred serpents licked my ears
and hid when startled amid the laurel leaves.
Ever since then I have possessed this gift like a mark of infamy
and fall into prolonged trances where I see only hatred and
    destruction.
I know I am heading straight toward death;
my shadow slowly drifts away from my flesh
and I see my bones being eaten by birds,
my mouth closed forever, my hands
plunged into the fateful boiling of blood.
No one will believe me, then,
though nothing will have kept me from telling this tragic truth.

Tiresias Speaks

It was on a steamy afternoon that I surprised Minerva naked at
     her bath.
In ecstasy I observed her radiant beauty and lofty majesty emerge
     from the water.
Approaching me slowly, then,
she lay her fingers on my eyes and closed them forever.
Minerva never knew the harm she did me
but as a result I can see in my darkness
the fire that consumes the heart of man.
I am Tiresias, whom they call "Diviner,"
the man who struck the serpent one night
and was transformed into a woman. I am Tiresias
the seer, whom they call "Child of the Night."
They say my greatest virtue is prudence.
I don't deny it.
The night has taught me to reveal only what is necessary
and to keep secret the fate that vexes and torments man.
How often have I borne their questions in silence!
They have called me the "Depraved of Depraved,"
accused me of deceiving innocent creatures
and threatened me with the brutal futility of fists.
Of course, my advanced age compels veneration and, besides,
who would dare assault a poor blind man?
My blindness is a shining bronze sword
that defends me.
I fix my dead stare where I sense their eyes to be
and affect a sympathetic glance, making a face
that must be as monstrous as the truth I conceal.
I grow impatient now and then and almost yield to the
     temptation of revealing all I know
but stop myself just in time.
Rather sorrowful, man's fate.
I swear no one will squeeze a word out of me.

Sermon on Death

In memory of Oscar Indacochea.
Unaccountably.

1

A vulture did craunch the poor man in the forest.
Ah! In what a cruel tomb buried he his limbs!
—ENNIUS, ANNALS

The pounding of a piano in a dark room,
flowers' fleeting perfume, the rock's rough surface scraping
    against our fingers.
How many things lie in wait for us when death is on the prowl:
the vulture's curved beak, its ungainly shadow and absurd final
    act.
Murky waters pitilessly pound the iron bedframe, toppling high
    walls and flooding chambers.
The king trembles.
His lackeys run off in search of shelter while the women
cover their children's bodies with rags and listen
in fear to their dogs' frightened howls.
Now they know.
The Beast of Our Lord rides hard upon us.
Oh, the purity issuing bloodily forth from the vulture's beak!
Pain laps our delicate limbs while compact
death unfurls in our bowels like a cruel seed.
Murky waters drench the bushes, cleanse rocks, polish our faces.
Murky waters dampen the bones of the bird
and its wet feathers take flight, swooping down blindfolded upon
    its prey.
The king trembles, but his realm is secure.
By tomorrow we will have lost all fear of death.

2

The tygers of wrath are wiser than the horses of instruction
— BLAKE, *THE MARRIAGE OF HEAVEN AND HELL*

So we sink our eyes into the swamp and feel our way along the
    mud's soft viscosity,
cover our heads with pillows and close off old balconies,
denying the lightning its bolt of refulgence.
So we accept that a solid wall can crumble to pieces,
that beyond the wall lies only rubble,
that beyond the rubble silence lies,
that beyond the silence rises the throne of Our Lord
with his pallid gaze, watchful finger and horrible baroque manner.
How many things lie in wait for us when death is on the prowl.
What we call *feeling* grows thin as our understanding dims,
mere shards of glass twirl in the darkness now
by a tiger's wise indignation:
a blind rage that conceals our resignation.

3

Poor Ophelia,
All those ghosts he never saw
Floating to doom
On an iron candle
— JIM MORRISON, "ODE TO L.A. WHILE THINKING
OF BRIAN JONES, DECEASED"

After the dust storm
and the unfinished cycle of the rose,
after the dream you've dreamt in the usual position,
the arrows have flown wide of their mark.
On the walls of a church the word *life* is obscured with manure.
Corpses pile up in the city while rats
scurry over the pavement, fighting dogs for their prey.

Trees providing no shade there
will continue not providing any.
I know these scenes,
liquor, a few plants, the fertile imagination.
How many things lie in wait for us when death is on the prowl.
A woman is swept away by the river,
tiny flowers entwined in her hair, her hands
lying folded on her breast. She's only sleeping.
Not even a fly is attracted by this candle's faint light. No book
can distract the heart from so great a sorrow.
Today someone beloved by her has died and she is at my side.
Ophelia is her name and she's only sleeping
beneath this flame's faint light.

   4

Wañuy pacha chayamunka
Konkkay konkkay tarisunki;
Kantapunin maskhasunki. A!
Kausayninykin tukukunka.
— WAÑUY PACHA, QUECHUAN PRAYER

Like feeling marked by the finger of God and running off
in futile search of shelter;
like walking peacefully through the streets and seeing in every face
an old face that once was ours;
like looking in the mirror and suddenly seeing
the skull's pale smile, the grimace of Our Lord;
like delving tremulously into the word and discovering
that trembling and silence are one, and despair one as well;
like discovering the hidden face of despair.
How many things lie in wait for us when death is on the prowl.
It's pointless to brandish youth, truth, ephemeral beauty, pointless
shrewdly to postpone the chess match and hide out on some
    deserted beach.

Death will know where to find us:
submerged in our own shadows,
happily drinking our final liquor.

5

La speranza si torce,
e ti attende, ti chiama.
Sei la vita e la morte.
Il tuo passo è leggero.
— CESARE PAVESE, "YOU, WIND OF MARCH"

The wind of March alights upon our eyes and shuts them.
Lightly we tread toward death,
a useless silence still weighing on our faces,
a heart-rending memory still burning in our flesh.
How many things lie in wait for us when death is on the prowl.
Bits of salt erase the word from its lips and its tongue
speaks to us of places we haven't been.
("Water" is what it really says
as water and mud forever flood the senses.)
The pain now lost, little else remains,
just a bird's pallid warbling as it ruffles its feathers
and a film of sweat on the back of the mirror.

Wind of March, you came bringing hope.
Wind of March, we'll never listen to you again.

6

Is it for this, that we die so much?
Only to die,
must we die each instant?
— César Vallejo, "Sermon on Death"

Moment to moment we age, defecate, wound the swarm of time,
    rest and read three or four books.
Moment to moment we kneel in church, take communion, enjoy
    a fly's buzzing past, blow out twenty or thirty candles, love
    one another, hate one another and make love.
Moment to moment a blade of glass grows in our hands, we drink
    coffee, listen to the record player, choose a movie theater and
    recall a few names with nostalgia.
Moment to moment a song dies out and with it a memory: lines
    from a poem we were given to reveal, the eyes of women who
    once loved us, the image of a lion crying behind burning ships.
    The fire of the conflagration.
Moment to moment words disappear as do children, loves,
    journeys and plans.

Moment to moment a little piece of death takes hold of us.

from *Songs of the Ark's Blacksmith*

Songs of the Ark's Blacksmith

For Carlos Contramaestre

1

One day,
finding myself below deck on the ark,
I decided to wipe the sand from my eyes.
"Unclean," they said,
but I was an old man when they murdered those children.
I was the ark's blacksmith.
I earned my living sharpening blades.

2

A knowing voice said to me:
"You'll be the ark's boatswain
and lovingly describe the living animals
while throwing the dead ones overboard."
That's when I became a blacksmith.

3

Some job, blacksmith,
scaring seagulls off the masts, firing up
the oven in the hold, fashioning
nails, arrows and crowns out of iron.
My lover is glad I have one.
Tough job, blacksmith.

4

It's night already and the rain hasn't stopped.
To kill time those on board tell stories
I listen to with my clay bowl.
They talk of warm lentils and speak
very respectfully of my older brother.
I never had an older brother.
Isaac didn't tell me.

5

Few know that Daniel,
held captive in Babylon,
bribed soldiers for a little wine,
frequented whores in the temple
and tamed savage lions in the circus.

6

(I have it from the lion himself.
On Saturday night we drank until dawn
and he blabbed like a drunkard
until sleep overcame him.)

7

Brief, like the life of an insect,
the old masters counsel.

8

Sailing along we came upon a dead man.
The women covered him with jewels,
put red makeup on his ashen cheeks
and sang like they'd never sung.
It's only natural.
They had never seen a dead man before.
Forty days are quite a lot amid the loneliness of the ark.

9

My father was not a blacksmith, but he was my father
so he sat me on his knee and said,
"If you want to be happy, don't be a blacksmith."
He died like vineyards do in winter.

10

The dove has returned on wet wings.
The blacksmith impatiently awaits it in its cage.

Films

For Patricia Villalobos and Javier Valdés

1

They were showing a film by Fellini.
On screen were clowns tumbling at daybreak,
delectable whores and cats
snoring on enormous garbage cans.
We made love in the streets of Rome.
She whistled absentmindedly as the clouds
slowly blotted out the treetops.
Outside the wind stood guard over the sleeping city.

2

They were showing a film by Buñuel.
On screen were black-clad priests drinking hot chocolate,
eyeballs sliced open and sheep
wandering through sordid mansions.
The lovely Catherine disrobes before a poor deaf-mute
while a man with a face of gloom
caresses a statue's white body.
She grabbed my arm and told me
please to control myself that God was
watching us from above,
lost in that dream's vacuous, pitch-black night.

Sea Stories

For Luis Jaime Cisneros

IN AN OLD, DANK-SMELLING ROOM

An elderly man leans back beneath his window
and gazes out weary-eyed into the empty space.
Beside him stands a table laden with medicinals, syrups
and a goose-quill pen
concealed between the brittle pages of a book.
That book recounts the story
of a man who lost his island's whereabouts
and sails around for years unable to find it.
"I was that man," the old fellow whispers,
and goes back to recalling his life beneath the window.

A FRAGMENT FROM CAPTAIN HOOK'S MEMOIRS

History is but a dust-covered tome, pages
a hand rescued forever from the abyss,
butterflies
the eye sees and does not see behind the screen.
Off in the distance I hear the surge of the sea.
How well I remember my pirate ship, my dwarf
servant's white sideburns,
that faun Peter Pan's pointy ears.
I remember, too, the crocodile that gulped down my hand.
Some day I will have to kill him.

IT'S TOO HOT IN VAILIMA

"Thar be ships sinking," the captain said,
offering me a spyglass so I could make out the crests
of tall trees on a mysterious, uncharted island.
His parrot pecked at kernels of corn and repeated

the old captain's words one by one.
"Thar be ships sinking," it said,
offering me a claw as if looking to take its leave.

Tierra del Fuego

The story goes that Magellan thought he saw bonfires
—where others saw only silence and sea—
shimmying like beautiful dancing girls
amid astonished penguins and snow-capped mountains.
"It must be the solitude," he said, "or else I'm going crazy."
He wasn't crazy, though.
Months later he would understand
that solitude is also a kind of shipwreck, the redemptive
spear that would fell him one sunny day.

Russian Legends
For Juan Gustavo Cobo Borda

TROTSKY SCRATCHES HIS HEAD IN ALMA-ATA

They call me Leon.
As with the old lion-king of fable
no one dares annoy me because of my pride.
When I was a boy they drew a Star of David on my forehead
which I washed off with blood so I could enter the story
where everyone plays a role without knowing how things will
    turn out.
Only I am aware of how the movie ends.
Burton is his name
and his sorry head a tough nut to crack.
Good God, it's hot in these parts!
There are even fleas here in exile.

IN A JEWISH QUARTER OF LITHUANIA

"The color scheme is all wrong. Blue
does not go with bright red and grandmothers
do not boil vegetables on green roofs.
Cows plant their hooves *on* the grass, you fool,
and that circus (Jews go to the circus?)
with fat women riders and everything just so dear:
the horse harnesses, the blazing fire of your hair
—torches in breakneck motion—
cut out that pink, it distracts from the yellow.
Painting is not your forté, Chagall.
Take up some other line of work."

Three Domestic Poems

POEM WITH DOGS

I met him in Istanbul.
A Turkish cigarette dangled from his lips.
He had beady eyes
and the fleeting expression of a ruined prince.
I never saw him again, but I purchased his portrait
at an auction outside of London.
My children go out of their way so as not to see it,
guests excuse themselves, making up all kinds of stories,
and even prefer not to come over.
My wife pets our dogs on the back.
She isn't afraid of them. Says they're man's best friend.

POEM WITH CATS

At night, before turning in, I read the Bible.
Only slightly moved, still I'm aroused by the story of Judith
cutting off the head of Holofernes
and the scene where the elders grope Susanna.
"Turn off the lights, it's late."
A feline claw bloodies my neck, sinking me
into the nighttime pleasures of love.
"Poor guy," the cat says,
"it really wasn't prudent to go off at this hour."

POEM WITH FLOWERS

"Time humiliates corpses," I told her
and proceeded to bury uncomfortable memories,
setting fire to her words one by one.
I love her and she loves me; some day
we'll float like buoys in the Thames

as we continue our game of cat-and-mouse.
I know she likes yellow flowers,
preferably roses.

Winter Lamps

THE ENGLISCHER GARTEN

We passed by the house where Paul Klee lived
and I recalled in hushed tones a few lines by Huchel:
"Your light is fading, defenceless leaves."
The park was covered with snow and silence
prowled about amid the black, bare trees.
We had our picture taken by the lake: ducks, swans,
roots pulled up for the winter
and children throwing bits of bread complete the photograph.

THE ROAD TO MITTENWALD

Through the frosted window
we could see the tranquil waters of the Starnbergersee
lighted by a pale winter sun.
The train stopped in front of the station and we looked
at pine forests, cabins buried in snow
and orderly tree trunks by a cattlepen.
"We'll never live here," you said,
and we drank a little coffee to warm ourselves up.

Christmas in Bavaria, 1986

1

It was Christmas with a stove and German carols.
The temperature fell below thirty degrees and smoke
danced on the window panes like an old ghost.
We drank toasts with Rhenish wine, listening
as sparkling Roman candles rent the night sky and wax
dripped delicately onto the tree boughs.
At twelve we threw more wood on the fire.
At one we went off to bed.

2

Through the windows
the sad smoke of chimneys appears.
I remember Christmas in Peru.
Mom would go shopping at bazaars downtown
and return with fake snow for the nativity and wheat
seeds to scatter beside the candles.
Oscar would set off firecrackers at twelve and my aunts
would shriek like mad from the fright
then laugh before shrieking again as only they know how.
I never liked Christmas, I must confess.
I don't know why I'm writing this poem.

The Dream Is Over

—John Lennon

1

A wounded horse gallops across the forests of England.
With silence at its back, a gunshot
rocks the wind and shakes the leaves on the trees.
Fifth Avenue, New York.
Dead flowers, a flame
and a few of the curious beside the bloodstain.
I saw it in the photographs:
dark glasses, wind, a little snow.

2

The needle on the record-player tears through the song
like an old dagger or shard of glass.
No one at the party dances, no one
hears the wind's groan breaking apart the night.
Observe the glasses in silence,
the shiny glasses free of liquor and rage.
In years gone by you drank to gaze into eyes
you now know are lost forever.

3

I read in a poem:
"Everything you have lost is yours."
Some possessions! A past that was just yesterday
and words I've erased then written down
only to forget again.
My wife comes in and tells me it's time to eat.
She turns on the radio and we reminisce about the old days.
"Everything you have lost is yours," I tell her.
She looks at me and smiles as if it were a joke.
I smile, too, before my food gets cold.

Lima Revisited

For Nilo Espinoza

"Don't Say It Was a Dream"

How deserted the streets are!
The gods have forsaken Antonio,
left him tightening his belt high and dry
in some lousy café. "Gimme a beer," he says.
Soon suds will cover his mouth and bitterness
invade his blood. This is Lima, Antonio.
The gods have filled it with the dead.

Night Every Hundred Years

We have inured our finger
to touching the most horrible wounds: death
dances among the scraps of garbage, shows
her sorry set of teeth on public transportation
and lifts her skirt to reveal
embarrassed genitals, newspaper articles,
banana peels
and the sound of the wind stirring up the night.

Men, Women, Boys...

Bare-chested men
unload sacks of sand or cement
and pile them up beside a construction site
while drinking liters of beer
on any street in Lima.
Stern-faced women
hawk their tamales, infusions, liquors
and enormous breasts heaving under the sun
on any street in Lima.
Boys at the age of innocence

eye the women lustfully,
smile among themselves and nervously
run after a ball
on any street in Lima, etc.

from *Remember, Body...*

The Conch and the Rose

So will I can do, in the dark of night,
Weary of else, deaf from speaking so low,
With the me, myself and I of my fright.
— Martín Adán

The lost roots of dreaming, affliction and mercy,
the never-ending moment when lips assume the earth's roundness
and lull it to sleep.
Call it surprise or amazement. Call it, if you will,
hope, the common ground where song rots away,
the horror of an age still speaking through your mouth.

...

You've broken into the coffer that safeguards the mystery.
For centuries you've coveted its verdigris film,
its sturdy pins covered with mold and saltpeter.
A faceless throng howled at your side,
calling out to you in fear during their long processions,
yet you attended only to the deaf conch's call.
(Place your ear on the deaf conch
and you'll hear the faint sound of bottles breaking,
the noise ships make when setting sail, their masts swaying sadly.)

Your fingers hold a Rose,
a Rose bloated with emptiness and abundance.
Up above uranium clouds cast shadows on the beaches.
No one is on those sands
for all have fled to the beating of a burnt drum.
Night levels sand dunes, uproots trees and redirects the rivers' flow.
It's pointless trying to see a trace of truth or beauty in them;
error alone starts up the world, error alone
plucks the air's strings, moving the wheel of history at will.
The wind pounds mercilessly at the walls.

What use is eloquence, mere words
that in days of old lulled lions to sleep, or poems extolling
    womanly goodness and beauty?

Up above uranium clouds cast shadows on the beaches
and you cannot stop looking at the Rose.
Its discreet stench moves you.

Love and the Sea

For Jannine

An ancient, timeless silence
amid the waves
— VICENTE ALEIXANDRE

1

I should make my way toward a silent door
and open it cautiously.
How useless experience is, years in disarray like feathers plucked
    from a bird,
the dirty scales concealing a delicate flesh.
No feathers or scales here,
no flesh, either,
just eyes shining in the middle of the night
and a nubile body on the red carpet.
(What is a nubile body doing on the red carpet?)
The wind scatters love's ashes,
sketching dying stars, shattered holes
and long psalmodies where a name forever blocks the way out.

2

To gaze at the sea is to gaze on a lengthy reproach,
to make the eyes glisten with words time cannot destroy,
to prepare to bear the bitter weight of years.
To listen to the sea is to listen to an age-old language.
Its foam is pure frenzy,
the airy transparence that makes lovers crazed with love.
You have given me eyes to see this transparence
because the sea is also a prolonged caress.
I learned this on drawn-out evenings of silence and extirpation,
evenings when love and solitude were not just words
but a vast domain where only you could enter.

To reach you I have stumbled many times.
I've spent entire nights counting your hairs one by one,
sloppily kissing the tips of your toes, imagining
your face in the faces of all women, your voice
in hundreds of mouths and on useless lips.
Yours is the voice of the sea, the voice calling from inside me
with its chasms and profundities,
its fish and waves and desert isles.
It's your body
calling me, compensating me for my error.

To reach you I have stumbled many times.
I've spent entire nights uttering a name, which was yours,
and entire nights caressing a body, yours again.
I've spent years patiently plucking a bird's feathers
to walk directionless toward a door,
not knowing it was you:
that ancient silence still speaking to me amid the waves.

The Fable of Ophelia and Segismund

1

The fair Ophelia! Nymph, in thy orisons
Be all my sins remember'd.
— HAMLET, III, I

If you stir the cold ashes with your tongue,
you'll see a crown of embers burning,
raging storms heralding the death of love
and a blue sword twirling in the darkness.
I had never spoken to you about that sword
but you'll recall that evening when the boy first knew the maiden
    naked and fair.
Dazzled, he fell to his knees
and, immersing his body in the waters, exclaimed:

"Ophelia, Ophelia!
You who are beyond all desire,
who have invaded my days and nights, who
set things in motion not moving! You seen
ruling the relentless pity of what cannot be seen,
let me drag your body down the river, let me
cover your beautiful hair with flowers and your delicate
womb with kisses!
Chaste Ophelia, rest your eyes on mine
so that I will know intensity,
that sword of yours cutting the thread and leaving me lost
amid the filthy towers of this dark palace!"

I don't recall what became of this young man.
His voice was a labored lightning bolt and his face
the flip side of a mask that knew no pardon.

2

It's dropsy making my eyes glaze
And brim with water now, I think
— LIFE IS A DREAM, I, II

A young couple walks along a riverbank.
A lone dog rubs his snout between the rocks
while the sun shines with its pleasing brightness.
This is the time for lovers.
The water revives its centuries-long melody and the algae
let down their green curls in the gentlest of currents.

There's hardly any water in that river,
but it doesn't matter.
Bathing is sacred here, the bodies
a cleansed indulgence in the presence of original sin.

...

"I see nothing but absence and dryness in your eyes, Segismund.
Hollow beauty has succumbed to opprobrium
and now you must face the inevitable alone.
For years you embraced a mirage,
furnishing it with names, verities and ghosts
until you endowed it with a cardboard humanity.
And so you built your ruin, Segismund,
because ruin is also not knowing transparency,
dissolving blood in a little compassion
and burying one's head forever in one's hands.

I should say that I love you, Segismund,
that for you I'd let my body be dragged off by the current,
fasten my hair with tendrils and thorns
and sing at your side on soundless nights.

No sacrifice drives me
but the sparkle in your eyes as they behold me
and your heart aflame as it glimpses my body's yearning."

Pirate of Memory

Voici l'écumeur de mémoire
— RENÉ CHAR

The time of those fallen in battle,
the time of geese in heat, the time
of the ax rusted by rain
has set me on the sad course of forgetting.
I'm talking about time that purifies memory by tarnishing it,
about ancient balconies slipping into the sea
and sinister little flowers the pelicans devour in moments of hunger
    and hardship.

I'm talking about the red star and the white,
about the day I conceived a child among scraps of garbage and
    mutilated animals,
about the sun that scorched two sleek bodies
then stopped to give way to the night.
I'm talking about the love that shines like a glass shard clouded by
    blood,
remote glass where eagles and hyenas burn as in a marriage bed.

I'm talking about the death of love and its rebirth,
about bosoms inlaid with rage
and long bouts in death's throes minus prayers and repentance.
I'm talking about spells of rain and shipwrecks, too,
about the son who killed his father one stormy night
and went mad in filthy town squares and far-off ports.

...

I'm talking about the red star and the white.
I've nothing to gain from remembering this but the pain of
    remembering.
The empty passion running through my days no more resembles
    sleep

than old age the tolerable resentment of the senses.
I fly without wings, spit in the mud and flip through yellowed
     volumes where others have written what I'm about to write
but I receive no reply.
I possess nothing but the word,
having lost all else in the shipwreck of my days.
I possess nothing but the word,
the word now slipping away from me, leaving me by myself.

from *The Bayard Street Tightrope Walker*

The Bayard Street Tightrope Walker

For Roxana and Jorge, who have seen them

He proceeds on tippy-toes, the Bayard Street Tightrope Walker,
his gaze avoiding the abyss as he rips all pretension out by the roots.
What good are heroism, grandeur, enthusiasm to him?
He holds life cheap, the Bayard Street Tightrope Walker,
cheap the indulgence of reaching the other side and repeating the
    same operation a hundred times over.
A woman watches him unimpressed,
strokes her children's hair through the window
and troubles his ears with her song, the Bayard Street Tightrope
    Walker's.
The neighbors pay him no mind, drinking beer from cans and
    conversing all hours of the night.
Who'd bother to notice so useless a prodigy?
Only the children point at the Bayard Street Tightrope Walker,
watching him in wonder, holding their breath and applauding until
    they scare the cats.
A Presbyterian church is the pride of Bayard Street.
Constructed at the turn of the century, it has a steeple and a belltower.
He sets his sights and advances toward the church, the Bayard Street
    Tightrope Walker.
His wife has prepared him a chicken leg, tomato salad and plate of
    lentils.
With any luck they'll make love tonight and enjoy a moment of fierce
    happiness.
She's pretty young, the Bayard Street Tightrope Walker's wife,
the one in charge of tensing the wire, the one who measures the
    distance between their window and the steeple, the one with the
    face of a heroine out of some romance novel.
He fears nothing, the Bayard Street Tightrope Walker,
although he hasn't slept well for several nights now.
They say he dreamt his shoes were hanging from the wire
while the children hoped he'd splatter his guts once and for all, the
    Bayard Street Tightrope Walker.

Raritan Blues

For Margarita Sánchez

There's no turmoil or hardship here,
just woods with wet trees and hundreds of frisky squirrels
scurrying about or poking at nuts.
Off in the distance there's a bridge,
an interminable line of cars returning home
and clouds bleating before a yellow German shepherd.
Is that you walking on the banks of the Raritan?
I remember a dismal brown river where rats
fight dogs for their own catch
and bored turkey buzzards delouse their feathers under the sun.
No turmoil, no hardship.
The river flows along educated, like on a post card,
and speaks to us as it has for centuries, freezing over and thawing out,
watching cabins, churches, brothels and oil refineries
pop up on its shores.
I listen to the Raritan's steady thrum, the silence of the ducks and
     enormous wild geese.
They've come from Ontario to New Brunswick
and will fly south with the first snowfall.
They say the river is life and the sea death.
Here is my elegy:
a river is a river
and death an affair that shouldn't concern us.

The Raccoons in Johnson Park

Returning is always a little sad.
Tonight I am with my wife and my wife's family
celebrating the birth of the Christ Child
in the stifling heat and humidity of Lima in the summertime.
Returning is always a little sad.
Soon we will head back to New Brunswick
where in all likelihood it has snowed and the sun will be a memory,
a cold crown of light illuminating the night.
(It's impossible not to evoke snow in the land of the sun
or silence in the land of fog and commotion.)
As I am writing I remember the raccoons.
I saw them once in Johnson Park:
gluttonous, mischievous and amusing,
they were cavorting rather close to the monkey bars,
displaying their cartoon-thief masks
and tails that belong on trapper-style, Daniel Boone hats.

Returning is always a little sad.
I'll see them again soon at the zoo,
rummaging for food in the garbage
or splattered by cars on the road.

Ithaca

For Javier Eduardo

Sometime in the future when they ask
where you're from,
don't hesitate to say "Ithaca." You come
from where everyone else is headed. With no Penelopes,
Argoses or Telemachuses around, your journey was
long and serene, I know, though you've had neither
the chance nor the means to say so except for your tears
and slight stammer: great big eyes
taking in the world
then three or four syllables we have forgotten.
It's this yearning for home that moves me. Because of it
I've traveled to many destinations and, because of it,
I've never arrived anywhere. You slink about
like a monarch in his realm
and aren't even a slave to your own needs.
I have traveled to be you.

It's spring, but snow is still falling in Ithaca
thousands of miles from the deserts of Peru.

River Rabbits

For María Paz

They are mischievous and brown, these river rabbits.
That's what I call them for lack of a better name: they live
in the clover patch between the road and bridge
in circular gardens where the grass grows
around a row of saplings planted by the community.
It isn't easy to spot the river rabbits.
They hide most of the day and in the late afternoon
—when the sun beats down upon the houses on Easton Avenue—
come out from the hills to sniff the lawn
and scamper through the miniscule meadow the city concedes them.
They are nimble and quick like all rabbits in the world
but, once they know they are being watched, stay quiet and still.

It's hard for the untrained eye to know they are rabbits.
They might just be scraps of garbage
or round, brown rocks lapped by the river.

Paterson

The noise of the Falls seemed to me
to be a language which we were and
are seeking and my search, as I looked
about became to struggle to interpret
and use this language.
— WILLIAM CARLOS WILLIAMS

The water, too, does what it can:
breaks rock when necessary,
carrying off fish, birds and tree trunks
while rising and falling painfully
like the womb of a woman about to give birth.
The waters of the Passaic also flow and break
only to grow calm again.
                              Look,
there's an old hydro station
and, in the river's pool, all the garbage in the world.
This is the language of the water. It rushes forth
in blind pursuit of a distant ocean
and repeats nothing but the same words to us,
words we will never understand.

Autumn's Defeat

Autumn is not welcome here.
                                    No one awaits it
on the bank of any melancholy river
hiding the world's secrets in its bed.
Autumn rules in other latitudes,
far off where cycles run their course,
where metaphors grow old and new again.

(The sun sinks into a greenish puddle
where a solitary laurel leaf floats.)

This afternoon, though, there was no rain. The leaves
cling to their branches,
struggling heroically against the wind,
and celebrate autumn's defeat during the night.

They don't know that the falling leaves are pages of writing
and the tree a dry, quiet poem minus the grooves.

Dream of Sirens

The insatiable fiction of desire.
— ROBERT LOWELL, "MERMAID"

I, too, have shut my eyes
and endured the leather thongs that strapped me to the mainmast
but could not keep clear of her black-winged perfume
or harmonic song blinding to the soul.
Because I did try to slip free.
Against my stubborn will I tried to slip free
and experience the frenzy that makes man fall,
the insatiable fiction of desire.
I might recall how her long flowing hair ensnared like a net,
that a sweet wickedness shone in her eyes, that her mouth
could lead me only to disaster or despair.
Her voice, however, was music to my ears
and her hands—dark wings that they were—
passionately sought to clasp my own.
I only ever had her in my dreams.
Sometimes I see her tail breaking through the water's surface
and listen to the mocking laughter I could never understand.
Then I pluck up my courage and swim to her isle.
There corpses romp about
before vanishing in a puff of smoke or turning into sand.
She covered the world with her eyes and erased me with a glance.
Now I only wish to awaken.

The Rain

I come from a city where it never rains,
where the sky is (as they say) donkey-belly gray
and the sea an invisible spiderweb enmeshing and blurring the horizon.
It's raining this afternoon in New Brunswick
and I've leaned out the window to contemplate other episodes of rain.
Like that one in Madrid, for example, when the water came up to our
    knees
and we splish-splashed along as if it were nothing,
or the one that caught us off guard in Tumbes
with its rafts and caimans navigating through a palm-tree forest.
And what's there to say about the downpour that destroyed Dante's
    tomb?
But that's a literary rain,
like saying it lasted forty days
or that it cries softly in my heart, which isn't true.

It's a different rain I remember.
Many years ago,
the water sprinkled the earth and formed a blue, mysterious mud.
That was silence teaching me its metaphors,
its laborious language once again smashing into pieces on the rocks.

How Poems Die

A mother's death
does not restore us to the world.
                              A father's, either.

It all depends on how you look at things.
While labor and management seduce their young daughters,
predators and preyed-upon unite to storm the heavens
and make the seasons' wheel turn round again.

It all depends on how you look at things.

Yesterday I saw a deer run over on the road.
It will be carrion soon, crow food,
a dark blotch on the pavement.

That's how poems die, my sweet Bambi,
like old movies we loved as kids
but don't bother now to remember.

Central Park

For my brother Carlos

It was not the best day to visit Central Park.
The night before it had rained and the grounds
accented the ugliness of a wet but snowless winter.
Still, it was our day.
We spoke of futile desires of the flesh,
of long-held grudges and forgotten friendships,
of insignificant incidents that time turns into legends.

The past shines on faintly
like the winter light in Central Park.

Then we remembered the photo.
It was many years ago, at a park in Lima.
An itinerant photographer asked us to pose
and we came out looking rather serious,
maybe because we felt lonely
or because we were onto something.
(Children are always onto something.)
Like the ones playing and smiling
in a well-lighted corner of Central Park.

from *The Water's ABC's*

Rats & Mice

1   LIMA, 1970

Children armed with brooms, stray
dogs baring their fangs and an old woman
screaming on the phone with the local police.
I remember its tail,
blackish and smooth like a light cable.
The convulsions, the flies, the worms.

2   MADRID, 1986

Swollen rat cadavers float
upon the river's surface. Befuddled
swans swim off to the side. Someone
passes the time by throwing rocks at them.
What can I say about their soaked pelts,
their open, sightless eyes, their long
journey toward the sea of death? Not a thing.
They're already dead.
Their fate is to rot in the sun
on the parched, brown Castilian plain.

3   SANTIAGO DE CHUCO, 1988

In the town
where Vallejo was born the streets
smell like damp earth, like just picked vegetables,
like fresh bread baked without salt or yeast.
We rose early
that morning to find eight rats
lying in a pile at our hotel door: eight
dead rats facing skyward
on a rainy day
in the town where Vallejo was born.

4 NEWARK, 1993

It looked like a dog. We saw it while
stopped at a traffic light. The creature leapt—God knows how—
down from a tree onto a garbage can. Its silhouette
projected by the street light above
combined with the shadows of the buildings
as the moon—
full like the thing's belly—
was scattering its white light
throughout the infinite dark blue skies.

5 SALAMANCA, 1996

My fascination with the storks
kept me from seeing the meek little mice
scurrying amid the stones of Salamanca.

Scrawling Crows

In an old Chinese poem I read "his ink can scrawl but crows." I take a moment to think about crows. I saw some this morning devouring the carcasses of squirrels and deer, cawing on the glittering snowbed (and they so dark, cawing on a glittering snowbed!), winged holes that words fail to reach. Once again I become absorbed with their being. How can I explain it? A dirty fluttering beats the snow, a feathered stammering that won't let me sleep. I think of Darío: "A great flight of crows stains the azure of heaven." It's not hard to see his plaint, his Golden Page streaked with the wild, savage creatures. Vallejo had his crows, too. So did Poe, so did Zhang Kejiu. In the Chinese tradition, "scrawling crows" means writing badly. I look at the glittering snow this morning and the flesh of deer torn to shreds in the beaks of crows.

The Carousel in Recreation Park

I sought a theme and sought for it in vain
— W. B. YEATS

The circus animals have not deserted their posts. They're still there, waiting for autumn to arrive, moving closer together to warm their hides by rubbing their coarse pelts against one another in hatred and resentment. I listen to their music without complaint, the repetitive, insistent player piano that so delights the children in Rec Park. A horse gallops over the rubble of Berlin after the bombing. I remember the screams, the collapsing buildings and the blood-soaked beats of a burnt drum. There has never been a bombing here. The birds build nests in the park, the trees offer their branches to autumn and the horses remain silent. Have you ever seen the horses? They're still there, pointless and beautiful, rising and falling to the rhythm of the player piano without offering the consolation of even the slightest desertion.

The Sound of the Susquehanna

Oneida, Onondaga, Tuscarora. What long-gone language named this river? What men and women found delight on its banks? What gods blessed its waters, uttering the secret word those residing with me here have never heard? The gods know it, though. They cross this water daily, not stopping to hear its opaque song, its ice-packed sound afloat adrift. I repeat those names in vain—Oneida, Onondaga, Tuscarora—and hear the far-off roar of battles, echoes of a past that has barely survived. I don't know what else to write about this river. I toss my sheet of paper and watch it disappear into the waters. There it goes, like history, like love, like our very selves.

Just an Average Dog

The cemetery in Johnson City lies very close to the town itself. Hardly a street separates it from the community of the living. Yesterday morning we visited its hills. Dry leaves rested upon marble tombs and squirrels scampered amid the crosses (Lutheran and Catholic— its's all the same to squirrels). There were mausoleums, some circumspect but elegant, others proud but modest. The sky was clear (that's a lie) and it was a little windy. We saw old men patiently waiting for their wives, families enjoying afternoon picnics and even an artillery regiment from the glorious Northern Army. Our time there was short. We didn't pray for the dead or leave them any flowers. As we were going, a dog barked at us. It shot out from between the graves, then returned to where it had emerged, spooked.

Reasons for Writing Poetry

That's when I saw my parents. I can remember it as clear as day. She was watching us play through the window while he divided his attention between the television and the paper. Not only were they not dead, they were quite young (younger than I am now), and the day was disquietingly hot and humid, like summer in the tropics. I watched her take a bath once through the keyhole. I still remember her breasts jiggling slowly in the cold water, the light flittering of bat wings, the pained croaking of toads and frogs. Suddenly, I felt the swift and unmistakable thud of my father's hand. In truth, I don't remember whether or not he hit me. I only know that for one brief moment I possessed beauty and that, there and then, I lost it forever.

The Millennium Is Coming to an End

But the seasons are still changing, the earth continues to turn, and the fish open and close their mouths as they have for centuries. Somewhere in India, tigers contend for tigress love while in a nearby wood rabbits devour the same old plants and roots that nourish the soil. I should be talking about pollution and oil spills. I should be talking about indescribable plagues, about starvation ravaging villages or about children disfigured by radioactive fallout. Instead, here I am writing this poem, weighing its words, selecting them with love and care, with anger and resentment. I look in the mirror and see only darkness, a swath of empty guilt on the blank page.

I am writing this because I feel lonely, because words have abandoned me, because she is never coming back.

Monologue of Poet and Muse

Sing, goddiouss, say something, help me, don't act like you can't
    hear me.
I know you're there, snooping among my books, tossing me other
    people's words,
making fun of my poorly hidden impatience.
There now, come here a bit, scratch my neck, scratch my head
    like you did before.
Look, my hair is falling out and I grow grayer every day. I may
    not be so young anymore,
but don't you remember the good times we had
rowing boats, climbing trees, throwing rocks at swans?
You used to enjoy my squeezing your breasts and looking into
    your eyes like a lovey dove
for the world was ours then and you even overlooked my spelling
    errors and poor public speaking.
Oh dear, how things have changed!
It's twelve o'clock again and I've done nothing but trip over my
    own words.
They are forever young, though, jumping around, playing games
    and going all by themselves to the gym.
Only I have grown old without noticing how I have aged.
No,
I can't afford to despair. I just cannot accept that you're gone.
I don't want to go on being a root in the dark, repeating lines
    from Neruda I never liked,
which walk around saying this makes you sound conceited.
Come, come sit by my side
and see: my writing is getting worse and worse, rhymes pop up
    where I try my hardest to avoid them,
the musicality of my verse is now a horrid screech and I tailor my
    lines so badly
that the sleeves turn out longer than the collar requires.
Stop writing, then, and stop reading. That's easy for you to say,
    real easy.
I'll never take that advice.

Come, for I hear your breath heating my blood.
Come, for I hear your song off in the distance.
I don't care if I am to wait for you like a false promise
or to bribe you with the shabby glory of a poorly written poem.
You're on fire, hot with fever. Maybe you feel worse than I do.
I know, I know,
silence exacts a very high price and I couldn't pay it.
Don't worry, I won't ask you for anything. Just remember that we
    were happy once,
that we burned with desire in the four corners of the world and
    that we laughed until the earth spun round.
I know things have changed.
I'm not the man I used to be and you have nothing to offer me.
No matter, come anyhow, share my bed a while and lie to me like
    before.
Don't ever leave me again.

from *A Brief History of Music*

Dance of the Wind
(Anonymous. Berbérie, c. 1300)

Waiting for you yesterday
I cut myself with a knife

The blood clouded your silver looking glass
and made the rabel strings wither

You didn't come to stanch the wound

Someone
            (be he man or demon)
beat stubbornly on a kettledrum

Only the wind came
the solitary
            sorrowful wind

Brandenburgische Konzert N° 2

Fat rosy
       angels
frolicking
amid cotton clouds
           purple
stars
     and heavenly bodies
hanging on a silk curtain

In the background the chill
              the harsh harpsichord
the flutes
      the oboes
how much destitution they cloak
how much human suffering

In the background
         beggars
rub their fingers
pick up
    bread crusts
pursue
    the duchess's carriage
her lace
     fan
her tracks in the snow
Count the fleas
       in your bed
one by one
      the sleepless
nights beside the organ

Out there
             the wind
shakes the trees
the rain
             bores through stone
the columns of empire
tremble
             Nothing
will remain of these palaces
                              powdered wigs
golden
        forks
crystal
        vases
What ungrateful oblivion awaits them?

Fat rosy
             angels
drag their destitution
through the streets
                     sell drugs
fight
       the dogs for
a place in this world
What a world
                nothing makes it pretty
except the harsh harpsichord
                              the flutes
the oboes
             the fleas in your bed

your sleepless nights beside the organ

Winter
(The Four Seasons)

Stranded in the Venice night
a man
        grapples with the wind
cursing
        a wheel stuck in the mud
                        and furiously
whipping his obstinate percheron
The howling of a dog
                        slices through the snow
with silvery scissors
Everything
        grows fainter
the dying
        light in the street lamps
the Countess's
                unattainable
breasts
        the sound
of doors closing shut.

Once
        when I was a boy
digging through the snow
I found a penknife
a conch
        and a locket
With the knife
                I carved my initials
on a sycamore tree
                        I lost
the conch on a bet
but keep
        the locket on me

with its snipped curl
                    and the girl's
wailing grief at parting

(Her name was Nicoletta
petite and quite beautiful
she never
            let me touch her
but her voice
reached the canopy of heaven
with her white habit
                    and that sprig
of pomegranate in her hair)

Stranded in the Venice night
a man
        grapples with the wind
cursing
a wheel stuck in the mud
                    and furiously
whipping his obstinate percheron
The Countess
                    tires of waiting
wearily
        snuffs out the candelabra
and undresses alone
            as the snow
                falls
            the snow
                        falls
            the snow

Für Elise

It all seems
a bit sad
      to me as well
a
  bagatelle
a
  divertimento
for pale
      consumptive
maidens
and a young swain
         who
recites poetry
and picks
      flowers
from the garden
        you know the kinds
roses
    jasmines
gardenias
      daisies
forget-me-nots

First the glass of water
then
the sunken
      breasts
(oh
   the breasts)
and finally
      the pages
of a privileged
      book
of verse
   a cemetery

for yellow
            flowers

And the coughing
                    I forgot about the coughing
the bloodstained
                    handkerchief
the sweating
                the snow-white
sheets
        the overly stern
truly somber
                father
crying
        alone by himself
and a grieving
                    lapdog
that doesn't bark
                    or bite
refusing
        to eat
or drink

What else?
            The full
moon
        the funereal
piano
        the unworn
wedding
            dress
Who
        would have guessed it
Elise
        my life?

Grande Valse Brillante

Lace
    when I listen to you
I think of lace
white and
      transparent
like rice powder on the faces
of the most beautiful girls
And fans
hundreds of fans
        beating
air
  warm and
golden
like Spanish wine
like a red
    moist
mouth
   like a
red body
    like two
bodies
 sweaty
and flushed red
rolling at the foot of the hills

And shoes
    when I listen to you
I think of shoes
     slippers
with enormous silk
       bows
and a slow
   lean
     fervid

finger
        fervid
from such solitary
                pleasure

It's raining
            tonight
in the streets
            of Warsaw
The neighbors
            silently gather
their belongings
                and abandon
their homes
            kissing
grandparents on the forehead
and blessing
            their mountains
and farmyards
                and
blue
    meadows

Do you hear
            the sound of soldiers?
No one is left in town
just cut
    flowers
and flocks
        of swans
fleeing
    Farewell
farewell
        lace
            shoes

slippers
      rice powder
on the faces of the dead

Night on Bald Mountain

Obscene
        guffaws
murmurs
in a strange tongue
            They are still there
waiting for night
comparing
the length of their nails
             their hunched backs
the yellow parts in their hair
they come
        go
and come again
blotting out the sky
with their owl
        claws
and flying
        brooms
while in their midst
           the goatish Fiend himself
flaps his batlike
        wings
and wags his panther tail
shaking a penis
        frozen and stiff
like a bull's shaft
or a dowser's
        divining rod
On this midsummer night
          St. John's
eyes are mine
mine too the serpent
        entwined round his crozier
the scrubby ground
        and sharp stones

skin my hands
and the soles
                of my feet
If I had a lantern at least
I could see them
                dancing
so lovely to behold
                    so desirable
with no tulle to protect them
kissing his batlike
                wings
letting loose
obscene guffaws
                and murmurs
in a strange tongue
                They are
still there
        waiting as ever
for night

Russian Easter Festival Overture

First the window
          painted with flowers
then
      the branches
with green creepers
the blue
            vine shoots
and skylarks
Hundreds of skylarks
painted
on the leaves
                of the windows
put their beaks together
and sing

Cyril the monk taught me to read
sitting by me on the banks of the Volga
while he sang in Greek, Russian and Aramaic
The somber bells
                announce it's Easter
Sing with me
          child:
The somber
              bells
announce
            it's Easter
On the banks of the Volga
I met my first love
I remember her round face
blue
     eyes
and breasts
              small
as rabbits
              trembling

beneath her blouse
                    I remember
the grieving
                the heavy
iron cross
laid upon her blue
                        eyes
her round
            face
and the cupolas again
the teachings of Cyril the monk
the pairs of skylarks
painted
        over lakes
and mountains

                On the fogged up
windowpane
a solitary child
                uses a finger to draw
his alphabet
of bells

Le Carnaval des Animaux

Rooster syllables
                puffed up
pigeons on the banks of the Great River
pecking at bread scraps
                Skippy
kangaroos
            virtuoso
cello-playing swans
                opening
beaks of amber and snow
Snails and tortoises
                    houses on their backs
Whimsical
            frogs
leaping puddles
                on the moon dancing
their elephant pirouettes
A rabbit plays the piano:
                    plinkety plink
And now ladies and gentlemen
The Royal March of the Lion
                    The proud
beast sallies forth
                with his shabby mane
and uproarious retinue of monkeys
Passersby scatter terrified
throw themselves
                into the waters of the Seine
shout
for help
        Penguins
come to the rescue
                multicolored
fish jump from the aquarium as
octopi   sharks   squid

glide past
The telephone rings in the police station
brrring   brrring   brrring
but no one answers

A madame faints in the Bois de Boulogne
                A bemused duck
finds a fake beauty mark on her breast
a pearl necklace
                a love letter

Long-eared personages
parade behind the Legion of Honor
while greasy-fingered children
throw fistfuls of popcorn

                Quel scandale
the hens
            take flight
Those not reaching foreign soil
build nests on Paris rooftops
                Quel scandale
my love
            close the window
the *carnaval* is over
                    the record
has ended too
In the police station
the telephone   brrring   brrring   brrrings

but no one answers

Gnossiennes

Tous mes ennuis sont venus de là

Slow bubbles
iron-heavy
glum
    slow
glum
each looking at
              the others
joylessly
      reflecting light
like the creaking
of bones
wrapped in velvet
knocking at doors
             and windows
Look
    inside you won't
see a thing
only slow
      bubbles
iron-heavy
cold
    hot
cold
like mute
      tongues
on a blank sheet of paper
word   silence   word

Keys
flee the piano
      hide

in the oven
        and closet
and under the bed
          Keys
flee
Oh their nostalgia for tree
           and elephant
flocks
of elephants
        and musical forests
like in old movies

In the distance
        a masked man
whistles iron
        bubbles
tidies rows
of toothless coffins
and laughs
        seriously laughs
with not a thing to say
not a thing
       to say
not a thing
to say
     not a thing

Daughters of the Lonesome Isle

Do we have a mythology?
Would we know what to do if we had one?

Alexander
       cut
the knot
        and then moved on
The most aged there
            listened to bells
howls
     black
rocks
    and the razor's whish-whoosh
over a bristly
expectant cheekbone
           The Emperor's
widow summers
in the Babylonian isles
          a sandal
     floats on the sea
We never
should have begun
         this game
dizzying
     coins
pierce
    through the void
and hit
     the holes in the zeroes
the Kyoto moon
        the stupid
womb
do you like the glass of milk?

Alexander's
            blurry
indistinct
            image
the pane of glass
                  scratched by snow
here
      there never was any snow
just rotted
            timber
a faint
        smell of the sea
of Socotra
            grapes
I don't
        understand the signs
In Pomona
            you asked about the lake
        a lake
                is a lake
is a lake
        turn off
the lights
        already
close
      your eyes
and listen
            listen
listen
      again

Sacred monkeys
                  toss fruit rinds
saying ZERO
            in their garbled

tongue
      erasing
the words of Buddha
                  with their feet
a sandal
         floats on the sea
Only the most aged there remained
the others
           consumed by fever
ordered rain
            in their delirium
from the musician
                whom they hanged

before plucking out his eyes

from *Written in Missoula*

Poet's House

There, at that old desk,
Dante wrote his *Divine Comedy*.
This is where he used to walk,
stoking the fires of the inferno,
looking for something to eat in the pantry
while threading together a tercet.

I cried in Dante's house.
It was the day Firenze beat Juventus 1-0.
The sun bathed the hills in golden light and the waters
of the Arno flowed, unwittingly, beneath the Ponte Vecchio.

A little old man selling souvenirs
told us (in very hushed tones)
that Dante had never set foot in that house.

And at this I was mildly abashed.

Buffalo

In days of old, buffalo dotted the plains
with a soft, light brown.

Their hooves fearlessly trampled these pastures.
This was their home, their vast
dominion no one dared profane.

In the summer
they migrated north, where the sun dies down,
and in the winter headed south
where the stars subside.

I saw some buffalo on our way to Montana,
distant, mythic buffalo awaiting a stampede,
a cackling of birds, a war cry.

If there was ever a God in these lands,
He would have had the head of a buffalo.

The St. Ignatius Indian Mission
(Montana, 1854)

The Jesuits made it all the way out here.

This is where they built a church, a couple of cabins
and two or three schools.

They preached tirelessly in these precincts,
looking, as always, toward the east.

Here, from this river, they drank other waters, gave names
to other waters still and spoke other tongues.

This is where they learned about demons who were gods
(sad, discredited gods,
but fearsome and just all the same).

This is where I returned to high school on the sands of Peru,
way down there where the Jesuits made it, too.

The Color of Nightfall

Orange nightfall
                 with its fraying clouds
and sun illuminating every word.
A gas station's logo features a dinosaur
(there used to be dinosaurs here)
and an endless plain.

Where did I learn all this?

Let's put aside the clouds for now—they're always
the same. Let's put aside the sun, too,
easy prey for every metaphor.
That leaves us with the orange.

Some say the orange came from India
where it was food for the gods
and others that it came from Persia or Arabia
along with its name and color.

Virgil called it *aurea mala*
and dropped one into an eclogue.
Holding the fruit in his hands, Columbus
discovered that the world was round
and that by traveling west
he would (like the sun) reach the east.

Now we are alone, the orange and I.

It has taken centuries to say "orange nightfall."

Mortally Wounded Okapi

For years now, I have been hounded by the title
"Mortally Wounded Okapi."

I must have read it somewhere as a kid,
flipping through the pages of an album
or the illustrations in an animal book.

I can still picture the scene:
the swipe of the cat's claw,
                    a backdrop of acacia trees
and the terror of the victim
in its futile attempt to flee.

Strange animal, the okapi —
not quite zebra, not quite giraffe, timorous
and nocturnal, in danger of extinction.

When I went to see one at the Berlin Zoo
it approached me off that far-away page
and said, so that no one else could hear it:

"I'm still mortally wounded."

Bears

For Christine Wilcox

In this city dedicated to the bear,
I haven't seen a bear yet

except in the airport lounge
where one such specimen is stuffed.

Do you know the story?

It was found near Port Heiden, Alaska,
where a hunter had left it
as food for the birds.

A merciful soul
restored it to a frozen pose
with a ferocity in which Time
(and every season) forever stands still.

Silent in its glass display case
the bear awaits the hunter's return.

It knows he will come. It's waiting for him still.

The Cat and the Moon

When two close kindred meet,
What better than call a dance?
— W. B. YEATS

The neighbor lady's cat arches its back
like the arc of the moon.
       The moon
licks her whiskers like a cat
and wails for a saucer of milk.

The neighbor lady watches TV
(she doesn't wail)
then creeps through the grass,
inventing new dance steps.

Cheshire Puss or Minnaloushe,
        the moon
will hold out her hand to me tonight
and I'll tell her (with ever-changing eyes):

"I'm sorry, but I don't like to dance."

To Reach Missoula

Years ago I read
a poem by Robert Bly about Missoula.

I can still remember it
                        telling of a train
(maybe from the old Pacific line)
that was traveling on a winter morning. The sleepers
had left the dark shadows behind
and through the window,
                        covered with streaks of snow,
they could glimpse the contour of the mountains.
You used to need snow to reach Missoula,
to pass through "Hellgate"
as the settlers called it in days gone by.

We arrived here by car
on a summer afternoon. It was really sunny,
so why did the chill of the poem still chase us?

To reach Missoula
you used to need a train,
a frost-covered window and at least light snow.

from *The Faker*

An Afternoon in the Prado Museum

"Atalanta and Meleager" by Rubens

Proud Atalanta picks gold apples up,
so though the race is lost, a suitor's won.

"The Drunks" by Velázquez

Since Dionysius lost his satyr chums,
he bides his time in boredom with old drunks.

"Phaeton" by van Eyck

To steal a carriage, Phaeton, seems inane
when one could take the stairs or flying trains.

"Achilles Discovered Among the Daughters of Lycomedes" by Rubens

Achilles, dodging war against Troy's troops,
dons women's clothing and a heap of jewels.

"Vulcan's Forge" by Velázquez

Lame Vulcan strikes his forge and fire roars
while faithless Aphrodite drops her drawers.

The Cemetery

The angel of masturbation licks my shoulder,
tosses his marriage flower at my feet and sings full-throatedly:
"Your first love is lost forever."
I don't listen to him.
I spent the night dreaming I was visiting a cemetery.

I had argued a long while with my girlfriend.
She wanted to visit her sister's resplendant corpse
and I my cousin's despondent one.
After two hours we reached this agreement:
we would go see her sister and her entire family,
but in return I could hide where the wake was being held.

What a great feeling to touch oneself amid the fading, wilted
    flowers!
I should be clear that there wasn't really a wake. The cemetery
    looked like a garden
or some lovely citadel where husbands might take their young wives
    for walks,
feeding dogs that barked without the slightest respect for the dead.
The young wives, meanwhile, dreamt of returning home to pull
    down their husbands' pants
as the husbands still felt desire for them,
pinching their rears behind the hedge encircling the graves
and jumping for joy as if seeing their tiny breasts for the first time.

Not much could be seen through the window.
Maybe the breath of the dead, I told myself,
or the faint frost on the hospital's glass panes.
Then I saw my grandfather.
He seemed on the verge of climbing out of bed,
his gentle eyes still heavy with sleep, his hair
slightly dishevelled, his pajamas white with blue stripes.
"Grandad," I shouted, "I'm here!"
But he didn't notice me at all.

I should say that the day was clear and bright
with cloudless skies and a sun as shiny and solitary as the pupil of a
    one-eyed man.
It felt like a Sunday, but the Lord was not in any of their faces:
no one prayed, no one seemed distressed, no one
dragged his feet as if carrying a cross.
I took my girlfriend to visit her sister
and she brought along a collection of photos she had inherited from a
    great-aunt.
She entertained me with them until her parents grew bored and went
    off to bed.
But that's another story.
We lay down without a word on the sofa, kissed each other on the lips
and, just when I was feeling aroused, she took out her great-aunt's
    photos again.
It really was perverse of her to show them to me one by one!
I looked at them entranced, nodding my head
as I felt the jiggling of her breasts, elusive as hares fleeing a pack of
    menacing hounds.
One day I fell asleep looking at the photos,
but that's another story.
In my dream I dreamt I was killing my ex-wife
and that, instead of burying her, I set fire to her underwear.
The smoke rose threateningly until it blacked out the sky
and I understood that I was married to the night.
"Your first love is lost forever,"
the angel sings,
while I, bored, roll over to the other side of the bed.

from *No Nightingales on My Finger*

Seven-Line Poem

Let's see if you can, she said laughing.
                              Tonight
the foxes will emerge in search of food.
The cold will blanket the streets with snow and no one
will sing, no one will see the dance of the dead
or the south ablaze in the mornings. The flower,
rejected, in blossom again.

Let's see if you can, she said weeping.

Blank Sheets

What lies in store for us on blank sheets?
What veiled word awaits us there

with wedding gown and roses, letters

already penned, ashes and dust?
What's there to write when you're waiting for me

alone and in silence?

With My Shadowy Mouth

I will kiss your feet then
with my shadowy mouth
—JUAN GELMAN

Fear is powerless against water: water
is time, it is sand in the hands of death.

The flame we forget but the ashes remain.
Memory is like that. The sand, water, lips and death

you visit before going away, leaving me your name,
a blush I kiss with my shadowy mouth.

Not Even Hands

It's something how words rot away
when not a soul utters them, when

they traverse the tongue and strike
the lips. Words can strike hard, too,

when not a soul
uses them, when eyes
tired of telling lies close

and no one can open them, not
even hands that are
eager but useless. What do hands
know about words anyway, words
we wait for but never come?

It's something how words rot away.

Dry Leaves, Snow

Yesterday evening snow fell
though autumn isn't over yet. Now
they reside together, not touching: dry leaves, snow.

I don't need ears to hear or eyes
to see. I'm focused on that odd
couple that will remain paired maybe a night
or two at most. To whom

does the silence belong?
                          The snow
imposes its whiteness on the leaves,
pouring forth its light without expecting a reply.
The leaves

stand out in bold relief, rustle timidly
and are swept away by a wind
that drops them like gifts on the snow.

An odd couple, dry leaves, snow.

La Solitudine

"I'm sad, and yet the day is so beautiful."
Once again I read this poem by Saba.

Winter in his eyes becomes spring:
the birdsong unsettles the snow,
the ribbon of sun for which my eyes are grateful.

I don't know whether I ought to be sad today, but

only in my heart is there rain. Why
am I writing the word *heart*? I've never

written the word *heart* before. Still,
I ought to write it in the name
of love that is imperfect, in the name

of love that strolls through the streets and leaves
without caring whether the day is beautiful. Or not.

Horacio Morell

How much of your shadow lives on
in my own! How much light remains
to brighten those eyes that come to me

in the night and say:
you aren't what I wanted you to be.
      You are
who I was so that you could be, even though people
confuse us at times, like taking the son for his father,
though some of me at times
might glimmer in your eyes,

those cloudy, tired eyes
that don't in any way resemble mine.

No Nightingales on My Finger

The breeze leaves its breath behind, shining
beneath a purer light. Language
is condemned to be voice,
outliving us thus, a wet silent tongue
with the sound of birds howling, like a ship
lost on a sea of words. I don't

know what to sing. I am the others. I hope
the others are me. Like the trees.
I don't know what to sing,

no nightingales on my finger.

from *The Smoke of Distant Fires*

A Theory of Sight After a Poem by Seferis

Θερινὸ ἡλιοστάσι, ΙΑ´

1

i looked at you with all the light and the darkness i possess so
ends one poem and begins another or is it perhaps the same one?
i've never been to greece never breathed in the breeze off the pine trees
the monster is dead its stench overwhelms the beaches its light
brings with it other skies other equally blue seas yet that sea
is very far away it covers this page with ash and darkens my mouth

2

looking absent light is an art i learned as a child i would squeeze
my eyes shut until they hurt until i forgot who i was how
lovely the woman in black would say while the woman in white
would sit me on her knees cover my ears so i couldn't hear
and teach me to read too much light can darken things she'd say
be careful of the brightness when you're writing alone absent light

3

the poem speaks of something else it speaks of the sea they call
tranquillity of how far down a beautiful island goes of the warm
breeze gliding over your skin of an octopus
speared in the shallow sea of its ink darkening
the water of eternity that precedes beauty

4

we share bread and salt we share the ax
that chopped down the tree share the table the flowers
the music we listen to falling asleep is the same we hear
upon waking our mountain is not from aegina the pines
grow drowsy how should i look at you?

5

the woman in black said in olden days people believed
light to be rays that shot forth from eyes seeing
meant naming the world shunting aside its darkness the woman
in white said in olden days people believed light
blurred the outlines of objects making them transparent
until they became invisible i asked her how that was possible
she said you write poems how is it you don't know?

6

will i ever scale that mountain dance beside the pine
trees feel the bitter taste of that salt in my mouth

see the octopus's ink panting in the foam
or the light of this poem darkening the sea?

7

no the woman in white said your duty is to write whether
or not the sun shines to touch the back of mapmaking to submerge
yourself in the octopus's ink and look if that's possible look but
not see yes the woman in black said your duty is to remain silent
    whether
or not the sun shines to twist your tongue inside your mouth to
    embrace
pleasure and not to write if that's possible not to write

8

i've opened the book in the summer solstice
its pages give me back a voice that's not mine
yet knows intimate things about me listing my
defects one by one i question it to no avail that voice
preserves within it a lock of blonde hair the token
of a forbidden love a concerto by tchaikovsky

the precise time of my grandfather's death whole
pages i had erased and written i said to it you win
what do you want from me?

9

some rays come from the sun some from the eye
creating objects by touching them when you sleep the world
disappears when you wake it sinks into the cesspool where
it goes i couldn't tell you ask leonardo ask paracelsus ask him
the eye is a geometry of circles a planet that spins around
without a care without stopping to observe the sun how turbid
the sun looks covering this page with ash darkening my mouth

10

they're always the same the blue sea aegina's dust the octopus's
ink leaving a puddle in one's voice or on the sheet of paper always
the same though the scene change the dream or desire
though beauty say no and truth shut its eyes

i look at you with all the light and the darkness i possess

The Book of My Life or My Conversations with Saint Teresa of Ávila

For Pepa Merlo and Álvaro Salvador

I don't know whether I am doing right
to enter into such trivial details

1

i write so as to save my life so that you'll forgive me i write
always my quill pen flying always looking heavenward always
at the ceiling his mouth can come out of nowhere
it's fearsome that bright shadowless flame of his that's how
he appears how he seduces i don't allow myself to be deceived
    throw holy
water at him make the sign of the cross but let's talk about you do
    you know
that music by heart have you read every book yet i was about to
    continue
the flesh is sad but i know whence you come for me you won't be
    able
to deceive me try as you like you won't be able to deceive me

2

the sound precedes the word so go ahead then draw
the word the sound comes with the music i don't understand
take some cotton and make a sheep paint
its eyes she said paint its fear its tail its ears
i was so nervous i didn't know what to do suddenly
it bleated suddenly it skipped about i remember that music
the teacher's horror the punishment from my parents the boy
i was has died she said learn this is a poem

3

yesterday as i was praying the devil sat on my book
get thee hence i told him his smell is so strong i want to be alone
he told me i have visions too i see ants tumbling headlong

[148]

into fire a lion in the throes amid the flames i told him
you don't know it but that image is yours my road does not lead
to beauty i seek the truth he did not say to me you will die
for beauty's sake i will rot forever in the truth

4

with the creep of a lizard and the cunning of a monkey
with a cat's shrewdness and a crow's discretion that's
how he appears trampling me his claws scratching my shoulders
he blows into my ears i bite my lips until they bleed he calls me
by my name i don't turn around the face of death is abominable
yet ever so lovely

5

come nearer and tell me again that story with the cotton
balls i was to fashion a sheep i was only a boy couldn't
read or write suddenly it jumped off the sheets of paper
ate from my hand its music drowning out the words
there were no words it skipped about in the gardens sniffed
flowers felt such great fear the lion it occurred to gregory
his lion was an ant that perished for lack of prey

6

yesterday as i was praying i saw a fierce battle the demons
were fighting the angels i didn't understand the vision
birds dragged their bodies along like serpents saying in their language
that there is no place for angels that demons don't exist
the serpents curled around my neck saying in their language
you will not go to any heaven not dwell in any hell i
closed his book trembling from the love of god

7

why are you talking about angels? i've never seen one ever demons
have visited me though they ought to have she says but i don't listen
she writes about minor things trivial details is what she calls them
i stand by my language it's pointless there is no language
the lion in the throes the sheep dancing on pink cardboard

8

i can't leave much as i'd like to i've waited ages to see you
look at my feet all red my hands swollen from all that
praying and praying look at the clouds my girlhood distraction
i convinced my brother we wanted to be free run away from home
see the land of the moors they killed my brother in the south
it was so long ago i can't remember his face have forgotten
his name

9

it's hard to live with a saint who writes her quill pen flying sees demons
converses with angels yesterday i dreamt i was in galilee
saw christ jesus enthusiastic crowds surrounded him i could
hardly see him there alone with desert all around me
hollow lights piercing my soul and an abominable black imp
burning my hay for kindling i don't understand you should be clearer
the sky is gray at dawn blue when there is sunshine orange
in the evenings don't be fooled the sky is always blue
and he is legion that's his name he can come out of nowhere
tonight i'm afraid stay with me tonight

10

with the creep of a lizard and the cunning of a monkey
with a cat's shrewdness and a crow's discretion that's
how he appears trampling me his claws caressing my shoulders
he kisses my ears erases the words from his book one by one
i don't know whether i am doing right to enter into such trivial details

Putting My Library in Order Before Bedtime

În piept
mi s-a trezit un glas străin
i-un cântec cântă-n mine-un dor, ce nu-i al meu
— LUCIAN BLAGA

1

such silence all about me tonight i listen to the rays
of the moon striking my window to my heart's pitter-patter
in my ear it's pointless to stare into space questioning the
soul the voice of dead ancestors they come back
to live on a little still to stay a moment
with us their silence surrounds me tonight we have
the music they say do you have the words?

2

there are no wondrous isles here no wax for stopping up
ears no mast to which one can shackle a body only
a sea without coasts a lukewarm cup of coffee the mocking face
of sirens i don't understand why you are talking about sirens
what you're looking for can be found in any supermarket in
industrial waste in the dogs that bark at the moon

3

have you ever listened to dogs barking at
the moon? in a poem by silva in a poem by leopardi
the night is left a widow singing a sad melody i'm lying
i heard them bark all night in heavenuponearth they seemed
frightened afterwards there was a tremor and the following
morning a rainbow appeared

4

deafness educates the eye teaches one to estimate without weights
or measures breaks up rhythms makes constellations spin around
you know that geometry is beauty but beauty is weak
it cries at the impasse in every labyrinth on every beach where
the hero abandons it they've seen it prowling around your house
begging for change sometimes calling you by name
eduardo eduardo but you never listen

5

when i want to listen i close my eyes it's very easy i learned to do
so as a child I see splashes of language achaean ships crossing
the bedroom helen of troy's skull which hermes showed
to menippus the rhinoceros shipwrecked in liguria what ever
became of that rhinoceros I don't know ask longhi or dürer
ask about it in venice the masks rot and rot away
moving obscenely over a dance floor

6

putting my library in order yesterday a verse came to me i don't know
why i remembered it i must have read it when i was young may-
be i wrote it myself only to forget it later its music
furiously drubs my ears which is the worst way to sleep
but the most advisable for welcoming a line of poetry that strikes
one's memory until it hurts don't worry it tells me
if you hadn't remembered anyone else could have written me

7

the night stretches on like the pages of a book it's no
use counting sheep one by one no use looking
out the window at the business of the world the dogs bark
at the moon the sheep cluster together shamelessly rubbing their
    hides

against one another don't care in what order they're counted i can't
sleep tonight helen has not come the rhinoceros chews
hay indifferent to the public indifferent to the dogs that
bark and to the moon

8

staring into space is no solution the foam has its
limits you can see wine flowing under the infanta's skin the
whale stains the ice's purity with its blood my head
casts a shadow on the paper darkens any verse you speak
of a common place the abyss where sheep die
the smoke above the departing train venus's turbid
defect you have the music can you wait for the words?

9

that music isn't mine it comes from far away from remote
eras from the first rhinoceros that dreamt of venice from the
book you once lent someone last night i had a dream
putting my papers in order i came across a poem that spoke
of silence i read it in romanian i've never spoken romanian
no matter silence is the same in any language
upon awakening i remembered a few lines and just one
question in whose breast will you sing when i'm gone?

10

don't waste time it told me that's a pointless question
and besides it has no answer

Letters that Arrive without Fanfare

И море, и Гомер—все движется любовью
— Osip Mandelstam

Tes lettres de chaleur m'arrivent sans faire de bruit
— Juan Larrea

1

no the sphinx doesn't want an answer she wants my blue face
my old face overshadowed by sleep overshadowed by
fear why have you come she asks i don't know how to answer
gazing ashamed into her eyes i see her mouth's strangled expression
her endless rows of stony teeth did you see what you came
to see? now go and when you come back bring with you a
burning stake a fistful of snow a freshly cut rose

2

black birds fly along the beach dead fish look for
the carcasses of seals and dolphins it's the same old story so
many roses wheedled by time so many tongues lapping
the rocks blurring the shapes of the enigma you don't know
there is no shape there is no enigma observe the birds
in silence admire their blackness their dark way of asserting
themselves by day they follow the stars' migratory pattern
the turbid precision of the tides by night they give themselves
over to dream and allow me to sleep on a white horse

3

the roots decide to come up for air bored by their confinement
by seeking shelter underground thrust all at once into the light
of all the vegetable immodesty a heavenly scandal indeed the flowers
celebrate this wonder leaves fall to the ground turn dark colors
renounce the gods' supreme favor what have the dahlias
to say now?

4

how should you speak if we barely listen how should you keep silent
if your memory makes us drowse how should you sleep if your tongue
returns us to the ashes

5

you talk so much about yourself you'll end up being another person
the sphinx said bored i don't listen to her it's hard to hear in the
    desert let
me tell you a story my father was a winged dog my mother
a blue lioness or if you like a rock a motionless pebble
devoured by the wind listen to the wind its harsh music coiling
round my wings look how her wings burn how they dazzle
my eyes cloud my ears over forever how lustily she laughs
chewing up birds in sheer abhorrence spitting out feathers at my feet i
pick them up keep them in a box feed them to my horse

6

one foot in the thickets the other pierced with stars that's
how the blind man was singing look at the cottonfields the black sea
furrowed with triremes with cranes drawing close to my pillow
destroying the pages of the book i never managed to finish that book
unfurl sails rid myself forever of insomnia the night was
dark that's what the blind man sang in marlin in greek plazas
in filthy foul-smelling moscow streets see him? the sphinx asked
mockingly me you can't fool me

7

if i utter a word she sets the word ablaze if i decide to keep
silent she makes my tongue rot if i look into her eyes she orders
blue in aramaic tugs on my ears wounds the air's purity
with her nails then waits how incredibly patiently she waits
this is how i'll blot out your eyes how i'll soil your desire

8

open the coffer the sphinx demanded you'll see mist inside
other people's words that keep you from sleeping no i said i see
snow tiny snowflakes coming together joining up with one
another only to separate later where did you read that she asked
in a poem by lucretius tied to his stake i've burnt in his
flames i am reborn tonight it smells like love it smells
like dead flowers her memory is indestructible now oh sun
sporting yellow eyeglasses sun wielding merciless scissors fool me
one more time oh you with that impenetrable lascivious gaze
betray my desire give me back the illusion of love
the word that hurts the word that kills

9

love wounds the eyelids lights a torch
on every finger raises worms in people's eyes tonight don't
talk about love the sphinx said i thought she was joking
i haven't come this far just to hear this far just
to see your fate is to capsize in silence to breathe
through your gaze that was the nicest thing she said to me the most
disturbing thing that night i had a dream two oxen
were plowing in parallel lines first one line then the other
it looked like they were writing out some maxim drawing a pentagram
that's how we create enigma they told me then the snow fell
and covered everything up

10

my heated letters arrive without fanfare you like
that line yes i recited by heart they are the birds that fly
along the rocks that look for dead fish the carcasses
of seals and dolphins no she said it's the snow that weighs down
your tongue until it bleeds the unbearable stench of the rose
the stake where bored words go up in flames isn't it better
to be quiet? yes i told her and started writing this poem

Notes

The title, epigraph, and line "Leonardo saw figures that were stains upon a wall" in "Food for Fire" are from Robert Duncan's "Food for Fire, Food for Thought," in *The Opening of the Field*, New York: Grove Press, Inc., 1960, p. 95.

The first three italicized passages in "A Hot Wind Blows Over Desert Dunes" are from *The seven years travels of Peter de Cieza, through the mighty kingdom of Peru, and the large provinces of Cartagena and Popayan in South America: from the city of Panama, on the isthmus, to the frontiers of Chile. Now first tr. from the Spanish, and illustrated with a map, and several cuts*, John Stevens's 1709 translation (London) of Pedro Cieza de León's sixteenth-century *La crónica del Perú*, pp. 12, 12, and 5-6. The fourth italicized passage is from José María Arguedas's *El zorro de arriba y el zorro de abajo*, translated as *The Fox from Up Above and the Fox from Down Below*, by Frances Horning Barraclough. Pittsburgh: University of Pittsburgh Press, 2000, p. 47.

The epigraph to section 1 of "Sermon on Death" is Fragment 141-142 from the *Annals* of Ennius, in *Remains of Old Latin I*, edited and translated by E. H. Warmington. Cambridge and London: Harvard University Press, The Loeb Library, 1988, p. 51. "Wañuy Pacha," the Quechuan prayer that serves as the epigraph to section 4, reads: "Off guard, inevitably, death/ Will find you, though you might have known/ That it seeks you and you alone./ Ah! That will be your final breath" (translated here by G. J. Racz). The epigraph to Section 6 is from César Vallejo's "Sermón sobre la muerte," translated as "Sermon on Death" by Clayton Eshleman in *The Complete Poetry: A Bilingual Edition*. Berkeley: University of California Press, 2007, p. 563.

The line from Peter Huchel in "Winter Lamps" is from "Der Garten des Theophrast," translated by Michael Hamburger as "The Garden of Theophrastus" in *The Garden of Theophrastus: Selected Poems*. London: Anvil Press Poetry, 2004, p. 79.

The title of the first stanza of "Lima Revisited" is a reference to Constantine Cavafy's "Ἀπολείπειν ὁ Θεός Ἀντώνιον," translated as "The God Forsakes Antony" by Evangelos Sachperogolou in *C. P. Cavafy: The Collected Poems*. Oxford and New York: Oxford University Press, 2007, p. 35.

The second epigraph to "The Fable of Ophelia and Segismund" is from Pedro Calderón de la Barca's *La vida es sueño* translated as *Life Is a Dream* by G. J. Racz. New York: Penguin Books, 2006, p. 9.

The last four lines of "Newark, 1993" in "Rats & Mice" are a slight variant of lines from José Asunción Silva's "Nocturno," translated as "Nocturne" by Alice Jane McVan in *Translations from Hispanic Poets*. New York: The Hispanic Society of America, 1938, p. 205.

The line from Rubén Darío in "Scrawling Crows," "Un gran vuelo de cuervos mancha el azul celeste," is from his poem "Canción de esperanza," translated by Will Derusha and Alberto Acereda as "Song of Hope" in *Songs of Life and Hope: Cantos de vida y esperanza*. Durham and London: Duke University Press, 2004, p. 91.

The line "I don't want to go on being a root in the dark" in "Monologue of Poet and Muse" is from Pablo Neruda's "Walking Around," translated by Donald D. Walsh in *Residence on Earth*. New York: New Directions, 1973, p. 119.

The last line of "Poet's House" is taken from Ezra Pound's "The Study in Aesthetics" in *Personae: The Collected Shorter Poems of Ezra Pound*. New York: New Directions, 1950, p. 97. The line in Spanish is a back translation of Ernesto Cardenal's and José Coronel Urtecho's rendering of the verse in *Ezra Pound: Antología*. Madrid: Editorial Visor, 1979, p. 50.

The epigraph to "The Cat and the Moon" is from W. B. Yeats's "The Cat and the Moon" in *The Variorum Edition of the Poems of W. B. Yeats*, eds. Peter Allt and Russell K. Alspach. New York: The Macmillan Company, 1957,

p. 378. Quotes from Yeats's poem appear in this translation.

The title "La Solitudine" is that of a poem by Umberto Saba. The line "I'm sad, and yet the day is so beautiful" is taken from *Songbook: The Selected Poems of Umberto Saba*, translated by George Hochfield and Leonard Nathan. New Haven and London: Yale University Press, 2008, p. 149. The partial lines "don't know whether I ought to be sad today" and "only in my heart is there rain," as well as the phrase "perfect love," are also from this translation.

The title and last line of "No Nightingales on My Finger" are variants of the line "Un ruiseñor ebrio aletea en mi dedo" in Vicente Huidobro's "El espejo de agua," translated by Jorge García-Gómez as "And a drunken nightingale flutters on my finger" in "The Water Mirror." *The Poet Is a Little God: Creationist Verse by Vicente Huidobro*. Riverside: Xenos Books, 1990, p. 7.

References are strewn throughout "A Theory of Sight After a Poem by Seferis" to George Seferis's "Summer Solstice" in *George Seferis: Collected Poems*, translated by Edmund Keeley and Philip Sherrard. Princeton: Princeton University Press, 1995, pp. 206-14.

The epigraph to "The Book of My Life or My Conversations with Saint Teresa of Ávila" is from *The Life of Saint Teresa of Ávila by Herself*," translated by J. M. Cohen. London: Penguin Books, 1957, p. 221.

The epigraph to "Putting My Library in Order Before Bedtime" from "Lini te," translated as "Silence" by Brenda Walker and Stelian Apostolescu, reads: "In my breast/ a strange voice has woken/ and a song of longing sings in me—a longing/ that's not mine." In *Complete Poetical Works of Lucian Blaga, 1895-1961*. Ia i, Oxford, Portland: The Center for Romanian Studies, 2001, p. 60. The last line in Stanza 9 uses a variant from this translation.

9781844715213